THE DIVINE 'DEL...
Bishop Hall of Norwich
(1574-1656)

David A. Berwick

Published by David A. Berwick
From whom copies of this book may be obtained using the following contact sources:
72, Turner Road, Norwich, Norfolk. NR2 4HB
Telephone: (01603) - 612206
davidaberwick@btopenworld.com
Also stocked by Norwich Cathedral Bookshop (01603)-218323
Printed by Barnwell Print Ltd, Aylsham, Norfolk (01263) 732766

Acknowledgements

My very grateful thanks are no doubt owed to many people. My debt to the following people is very substantial. Without your valuable time, advice and encouragement this book would not have come to fruition.
***Norwich Heart & The Harry Watson Bursary* - for financial support**
Jonathan Plunkett; Dr Amanda Goode, *Archivist at Emmanuel College, Cambridge*; Dr Martin Allen, *Coins & Medal Department, Fitzwilliam Museum, Cambridge*; Dr Francesca Vanke, *Curator of Decorative Arts, Castle Museum, Norwich*; Dr Alison Dight, Exeter College, Oxford; Ellie Jones, *Archivist, Exeter Cathedral*; The Dean and Chapter of Norwich Cathedral; Gudrun Warren, *Librarian*, Norwich Cathedral; Nigel Bumphrey, *Norwich Diocesan Advisor for Silver*; The staff of the Norfolk Records Office; Clare Everitt of *'Picture Norfolk'* (Norfolk County Council); Archant Picture Library; Richard Hoggett of *Norfolk Archaeology*; Derek James, *Features Editor*, Archant, Norwich; Paul Wellbank; George Allison; Owen Thompson; Anne May *for realising cover & page 80 in colour*; Kenneth Talbot; Terence Burkill; Phyll Hardie; Revd Simon Ward; Alan Kefford; Gill Hadlum – *Clerk to the Diocesan Registrar;* Paul Hurst; Peter Siddons; James Akehurst.

By using carbon-balanced paper through *The World Land Trust* in this publication, we are able to save carbon and preserve critically threatened tropical forests.

CONTENTS

Introduction   v

Chapter One   **1**
Birth-education-early career

Chapter Two   **15**
Priesthood-marriage-children-Royal appointments

Chapter Three   **25**
Waltham Abbey-The Netherlands-
Exeter – the *'Smectymnuus'* affair

Chapter Four   **47**
(1632-47) Turbulence-The Tower- the *'Delinquent'* Bishop
Wreckers in Norwich Cathedral – 'Hard Measure'

Chapter Five   **75**
Priestly 'retirement' to Heigham-final days and death -
details of Bishop Hall's *will*

Chapter Six   **97**
Bishop Hall's final resting place & an amazing discovery

Appendix A   **104**
Joseph & Elizabeth's children

Appendix B   **117**
St Bartholomew's silverware – a new listing

Appendix C   **124**
The exhumation Faculty in full

Index   **131**

Reference Bibliography   **137**

ILLUSTRATION CREDITS

Unless otherwise stated picture copyright resides with the Author

Page 9 – The Dean and Chapter of Norwich Cathedral
Page 14 – The Dean and Chapter of Norwich Cathedral
Page 24 – Hawstead Church: *Courtesy Hawstead PCC.*
Page 25 – © *Paul Whellams, Waltham Abbey Church*
Pages 32 & 33 – images © *The Fitzwilliam Museum, Cambridge*
Page 40 – *(Top)* Bishop Hall image © *Emmanuel College, Cambridge*
Page 46 – The Dean and Chapter of Exeter Cathedral
Page 51 – Bishop Matthew Wren: *Courtesy Google Images*
Page 62 – Image © Paul Hurst Photography. Used with permission
Page 74 – (Lower) The Dean and Chapter of Norwich Cathedral
Page 80 – St. Bartholomew's Church, Heigham, Norwich
    From Delves, E – *A Brief History of the Hamlet of Heigham*
Page 83 – Image © *Norfolk County Council Library & Information
    Service (Photograph: George Swain 1953)*
Page 93 – Bishop Hall Monument © *Norfolk Records Office*
Page 97 – (Left) *George Plunkett's Collection:* Courtesy of Jonathan
    Plunkett and (Right) *Norfolk County Council Library &
    Information Service*
Page 99 – *George Plunkett's Collection*: Courtesy of Jonathan
    Plunkett
Page 101 – Bishop Hall's reburial 1975: © *Archant/Eastern Daily Press*
Page 103 – The Dean and Chapter of Norwich Cathedral
Page 105 – Robert Hall's Monument: Courtesy of The Dean &
    Chapter of Exeter Cathedral
Page 107 - *George Hall's Portrait* - © All Saint's Church, Wigan
Pages 108 & 109 – George Hall's Cup: © *Exeter College, Oxford*
Page 113 – © Norfolk County Council Library & Information
    Service
Pages 117-120 By courtesy of Norwich Museums Service
Page 122 – By kind permission of Nigel Bumphrey
Page 123 – Blue Glass Ewer: *Courtesy of the Vicar and PCC of St.
    Barnabas' Parish Church, Norwich*

INTRODUCTION

As you read about Joseph Hall's life you are certain to realise what an exceptional individual he was, and what an extraordinary life he had! However, it is important that this humble biography does not detach Joseph's personal story, (however fascinating it was) from its context within the eras through which he lived. There were a number of extraordinarily fortuitist and protective interventions at critically significant moments throughout Joseph's life. He was most fortunate that his guardian angel was ever working so hard for him when needed! Did Joseph simply 'ride his luck' during these events, or dare we say he was actually destined to follow a holy and protected pathway? You may well conclude, (as I did after nearly three years research) that the evidence towards the latter view is rather compelling.

A window on the world of Joseph Hall

Queen Elizabeth I had already been the reigning monarch for sixteen years **when Joseph was born in 1574** and he was a lad of thirteen when **Mary Queen of Scots was beheaded in 1587**. Luckily, Joseph was spared living during the previous harrowing reign of **Bloody Queen Mary, (1553-58)** which had witnessed perhaps three-hundred Protestant victims being put to death. **By the late 1570s the first Non-conformist congregations** were assembling, and not long after **came the start of a Puritan movement forming from factions within the Church of England.** This development would have a decisive influence on the teenage Joseph when he went up to **Emmanuel College in Cambridge,** for it was perhaps the principal **Puritan teaching establishment in the country**. Sir Walter Mildmay–a leading follower of Puritanism – had purposely founded this college in 1583/4 in an endeavour to produce more priests who reflected his Puritan sympathies. The college had only been in existence for five years in 1589 when Joseph entered its doors. **In 1588 Sir Francis Drake thwarted the Spanish Armada in the English Channel.** Joseph was obviously moved by this deliverance for he wrote passionately about it later, preaching a sermon titled *The Defeat of Cruelty.* I think we tend to forget that the country feared that a defeat by the Spanish fleet **would bring an end to the Protestant faith, which had been re-established as the national religion with the crowning of Elizabeth I in 1558.**

In 1601, when Joseph was appointed Rector at his first church in Suffolk, Queen Elizabeth I was nearing the end of her long Reign.

Joseph in fact shared something in common with Queen Elizabeth, **for they would both experience imprisonment in the Tower of London. Joseph and Elizabeth Whinniff married in 1603.** That year also witnessed **the crowning of a new monarch – James I. A learned author himself he immediately, (1604) set dozens of selected theologians the task of producing a new 'universally acceptable' bible – de-cluttered of Romish language. The King James Version appeared in 1611.** In the second year of his reign the country would see the halting of the **Gunpowder Plot and the year 1605 and 5th November etched into the nation's eternal memory. Charles I succeeded his father as King of England in 1625** and decades of turbulence and religious unrest followed. Charles' antagonistic attitude towards Parliament almost inevitably led to the **English Civil Wars.** Joseph was mourning the loss of his youngest son, Edward, at the end of a year that saw the **commencement of the English Civil Wars at the battle of Edgehill in 1642.** The nation was set on a course of grim deeds, which saw its people thrust headlong into factional military fighting **between its King, Charles I, and Cromwell's 'Roundhead' New Model Army. Norwich citizens rose up against the intended arrest of their Mayor in 1648. Parliamentary troops were sent to quell the unruly assemblage, during which a gunpowder store was ignited. The massive blast killed forty people. The grisly outcome saw eight local men hanged as conspirators. 1648 also witnessed two women being hanged in Norwich for witchcraft. The dreaded Matthew Hopkins had brought charges against twenty women in Norfolk in 1646 and they were all found guilty and hanged.** Joseph, by now living in Heigham by Norwich, could not have escaped knowledge of these terrible acts. The fact that he made no public comment about them probably means he was understandably 'keeping a low profile.' **King Charles I, who had always pleaded his deeply held view of kingly precedence over Parliament, would pay the ultimate price with his beheading on 30th January 1649.** This grim event thus ushered in the **'Protectorship' under Oliver Cromwell,** until his death in 1658, when his son **Richard** succeeded him. He soon displayed his complete inadequacy to fulfil the role of leader. The interregnum was unravelling. Cromwell's 'reign' had been undemocratically enforced on the nation's people and it was never going to last. Sadly, Joseph died just four years before the **Restoration of the Monarchy in 1660 when the dead King's son, Charles II, was brought from exile in France to be crowned as the nation's King.**

David A. Berwick. Norwich, April 2012

vi

CHAPTER ONE

Birth – education - early career

J oseph Hall was born at 5am on Monday 1st July 1574 in the village of Bristow Park, near Ashby-de-la- Zouch, Leicestershire. Joseph was baptised on the 4th July. He was the second son of a large family of nine, perhaps twelve children; the exact number is in dispute. His father, John, (d. 1608) was in the employment of Henry Hastings, the third Earl of Huntingdon, who was based in York - hence he was also referred to as *The Lord of the North*. Not much else is known about John Hall apart from references to him having charge of the governance of Ashby, possibly sometime as its bailiff. However, as we shall see, John Hall does feature prominently in this chapter for he had to resolve the problem of funding Joseph's education after Ashby Grammar School.

We know a good deal more of Joseph's mother, thanks to the fact that he made a point of writing about her in some detail within his autobiographical tracts, particularly in, *'Observations of some Specialities of Divine Providence in the Life of Joseph Hall'*, (1647) which was written following his ejection from the office of Bishop of Norwich in the mid to late 1640s. It is certainly one of several books he wrote and had published during the last thirteen years of his life, spent at his 'retirement' Palace in Heigham, on the outskirts of Norwich. There will be much more to say about this very interesting extant building later, in *Chapter Five*.

His choice of using the words 'Divine Providence' within the title of the book referred to above was very apt indeed, as there were certainly many pivotal moments in his turbulent life, where, as we shall see, one could only think that a greater power was nurturing his progress and survival. His mother, Winifride, (née Bam(n)bridge) was from a good, though not high-born family, from the north of England. They had attained some importance in Leicestershire. Joseph's mother was a steadfast and devout Calvinist. This is what Joseph recounted about her:

> *"My mother Winifride, of the house of Banbridges, was a woman of that rare sanctity, that, were it not for my interest in nature, I durst say, that neither Aleth the mother of that just Honor of Clarenal, nor Monica, nor any other of those pious matrons*

1

aciently famous for devotion, need to distain her admission to comparisen. She was continually exercised with the afflictions of a weak body, and oft of a wounded spirit: the agonises whereof, as she would oft recount with much passion, professing that the greatest bodily sicknesses were but flea-bites to those scorpions; so, from them all, at last she found a happy and comfortable deliverance".

Joseph goes on to recall a description of a dream that his mother recounted to him wherein a man dressed in physicians' robes asked of her mood. She apparently responded in a dark vein, whereupon the image took her hand and told her that her depressive fits were at an end. After discussing this event with a priest, and after getting his assurances on the matter, she was content to believe that God himself had intervened and helped her. Every day thereafter she spent much time in thankful private devotion. Joseph relates that his mother was always a woman of great seriousness. Perhaps one should feel some sympathy for her, as she may well have had regular bouts of what we might today term post-natal depression. One can understand the physical and mental health consequences of baring twelve children in any age.

The priest she turned to was very probably the Revd. Anthony Gilby, who was vicar of Ashby and a leading local Puritan. Joseph was later to reject Gilby's views on church governance, although Joseph himself adhered to Calvinist theology all his life. Anthony Gilby also had some early influence on the young Joseph Hall, when the lad was at Ashby Grammar School, where Gilby was also the superintendent. The Earl of Huntingdon, who had engaged Anthony Gilby to set the curriculum, had founded Ashby Grammar School. The records suggest Joseph was tutored by a succession of radical protestant masters, chiefly William Bradshaw, author of *'English Puritanisme, (1605). The Halls close affinity with this school was to be further bonded when Joseph's sister Barbara, (b. 1518) later married John Brinsley, then headmaster of Ashby Grammar School.

As a child Joseph remembers his mother giving him serious instruction on piety, temptations, desertions and spiritual comforts. Such conversational subject matter betwixt mother and son would seem to us a bit extreme and daunting for a child to regularly endure today. However, it does seem in keeping with what we know was a dearly held parental wish from the very

2

early days of Joseph's life - that he should be prepared for eventual entry into the priesthood. In later years, (when this aspiration had been fulfilled) Joseph admitted that this steadfast, pure image of his mother had unfailingly accompanied him through all of his life's adversities - and he certainly was set to have plenty of them.

For all the stern lecturing in his formative years, it was generally agreed that the maturing Joseph had a remarkable and somewhat unique wit - a trait that was to manifest itself later as a vital component within his famed satirical writings. It would seem, however, on the available evidence, that we can be pretty certain that he did not inherit any propensity towards humour and wit from his rather awesome mother!

Young Joseph had done very well at Ashby Grammar School, but soon the decision would have to be made as to where his future education might be conducted. Not surprisingly, considering the size of the Hall household, funding this next venture would not be easy for his father John, who had recently been influenced towards a potentially attractive and less daunting financial solution to this problem.

College dreams nearly dashed

The Master of Ashby Grammar School had advised John Hall of a gentleman he roundly recommended as thoroughly suited to young Joseph's future tutorial needs. Joseph's higher education would be safe in the hands of the person he had in mind. The most attractive aspect of this proposed route was the lower financial outlay. The boast that this man could turn out a fully educated student, ready for the cloth, at a fraction of the outlay compared to a formal college education couldn't be passed up. John Hall was very minded to follow this course for his son. The decision would involve the fifteen-year-old Joseph being bonded to this tutor for seven years.

Mr William Pelset, (a Puritan teacher, lately from Cambridge and famed for his learning and oratory abilities) was to be Joseph's future tutor. Pelset was also Rector of Market Bosworth, in Leicestershire. Whilst all this was being considered do we know of Joseph's opinion on the matter? In fact we do. In one of his later autobiographical works he tells of his great disappointment at the prospect of finishing up with Pelset, for young

Joseph was keen to go to college. Desperate to intervene he turned to the Almighty and prayed for divine intervention.

At the very moment of his praying Joseph's elder brother, (whose name we are not told) came into the house on returning home from business in Cambridge, where a friend of his, a Mr Nathaniel Gilby, (a fellow of Emmanuel College Cambridge, and son of Revd Anthony Gilby, vicar of Ashby) had actually recently asked of young Joseph's developing aptitudes. On hearing from Joseph's brother how favourable they were he insisted that Joseph's father's consent should urgently be sought so that Joseph's higher educational needs might be met in Cambridge. John Hall, obviously warmed and impressed that no less than a fellow in Cambridge had seen fit to contact him via his son, had a complete change of heart, and declared without ambiguity that Joseph would go to college in Cambridge after all. Certainly Joseph was emotional enough to later admit that he was left: " . . . full of the tears of joy for so happy a change".

At that very moment, a representative of Mr William Pelset, (the would-be private tutor) called at the Halls residence, with a request that Joseph present himself to his master the very next day so that Joseph's education with him could commence without further delay. John Hall replied without hesitation that the caller should tell his master that the summons was some two minutes too late, for he had just decided that Joseph's future education was to lie elsewhere. A note officially declaring John Hall's mind on Joseph's further education was prepared for the messenger who was then ushered away. A dramatic and sweet answer to prayer must surely have been Joseph's only conclusion at this dramatic turn of events?

At this juncture, Joseph's brother again took up the conversation and addressed his father, (whilst on his knees, according to Joseph's later recollection) and tried to reassure him not to worry about finding the funds to sponsor Joseph, as he had come to a view on the matter himself. He was personally willing to forego any property rights that might come to him later in life via his father's will. In an act of great generosity, he stated his utter willingness to immediately have the value of lands due to him perhaps many years hence, realised without delay, with the resultant value placed into a Trust for Joseph. One imagines the young man must have felt warmly encouraged by this very loving and brotherly gesture. However, it is not known if this offer was fully acted upon for Joseph went off to

Cambridge in 1589 without any particular delay, and took up residence there in Emmanuel College. Accompanying him to Cambridge as fellow Emmanuel scholars were William Bradshaw, (his former tutor) and a close school friend, Hugh Cholmley. Joseph and Hugh were such good friends that Joseph felt obliged to comment; *" . . . as we had been partners of one lesson from our Cradle, so were we now for many years partners of one bed"*.

Emmanuel College at last

Emmanuel College, *(left)* was itself rather a strict Puritan establishment but young Joseph was quick to adapt to the new surroundings and his education proceeded well during the first two ensuing years. He simply must have relished an atmosphere where he could mix with and relax amongst other males his age and older. Joseph therefore had ample opportunity to develop a lighter touch on life for himself when circumstances allowed. His natural flair for poetic wit could develop and flourish within a new environment, wonderfully free of the doubtless stifling atmosphere of the family home. Mental 'detachment' would have been difficult within a house shared with perhaps eleven other siblings!

Financial crisis

Whilst separated for two years from his family and busily engaged in his education, his father had been struggling to find the financial support he needed for him. It will have therefore disappointed Joseph greatly to receive the depressing news in 1591 that he was being recalled home from Cambridge, owing to this funding crisis.

It would seem that things were so bad that his father had no option but to consider a financial rescue plan that would see Joseph's expensive education in Cambridge discontinued. The vain hope was for Joseph to go back to his old school as a tutor – aged just seventeen! No doubt John Hall would have been saddened to follow this course of action but his dire financial straits gave him no real alternative. At least Joseph could put his education thus far to good use and earn some extra money for the Hall household where it was desperately needed to feed some of those many 'pipes' as mentioned below!

Obviously the situation must have been discussed within the family for, right at the eleventh hour, a benefactor came forward to help. Edmund Sleigh of Derby, (Joseph's uncle) made the generous offer to underwrite half of Joseph's fees until he should attain a MA degree.

This amazingly munificent intervention was of course accepted and Joseph packed his belongings again and returned to Emmanuel College Cambridge. Joseph touches on this anxious time in one of his later books, recalling that he had been:

> "... fetched home, with an heavy heart; and now this second time had mine hopes been nipped in the blossom, had not God raised me up an unhoped benefactor, Mr Edmund Sleigh of Derby, [Joseph's uncle] (whose pious memory I have cause ever to love and reverence) out of no other relation to me, save that he married my aunt. Pitying my too apparent dejectedness, he voluntarily urged and solicitored my father for my return to the university; and offered to pay one half of my maintenance there, till I should attain to the degree of Master of Arts; which he no less really and lovingly performed. The condition was gladly accepted. Thither was I sent back, with joy enough; and ere long choosen scholar of that strict and well ordered place. My first two years were necessarily chargeable above the proportion of my father's power; whose not very large cistern was to feed many pipes beside mine. His weariness of expense was wrought upon by the counsel of some unwise friends, who persuaded him to fasten me upon that school as master, whereof I was lately a scholar".

In 1593 Joseph Hall duly graduated Bachelor of Arts. The aspirations of his parents were starting to be fulfilled.

Fellowship calamity

When, in 1595 the time approached for Joseph Hall to be raised to fellowship, a rather unusual, not to say unfortunate, circumstance came into

6

play, which must have put a severe strain onto the undoubted close collegiate friendship that Gilby and Hall had thus far established and enjoyed. Owing to a strict rule set by the founder of Emmanuel College, (Sir Walter Mildmay in 1584) Joseph actually found himself to be ineligible for fellowship on the grounds that only one scholar per county, at any one time, could be admitted as a fellow. Joseph and his tutor Nathaniel Gilby were from the same county! However unintentionally, Nathaniel nevertheless barred his way.

When John Hall's employer, (the Earl of Huntingdon, and a benefactor at Emmanuel College) heard of this situation he thought it preposterous and, in order to promote Joseph's claim, decided to wield some of his undoubted influence. He sent word to Gilby that he should travel to York where the Earl would speak with him about the 'Cambridge crisis'. It is unlikely that Gilby would have guessed the outcome of the audience at York, for Huntingdon, intent on tempting Gilby away from Cambridge, offered to create a new post for him as his personal chaplain. The promise of an attractive allowance was made plus the assurance of promotion in due course, should all work out well.

Whether Gilby had regrets at this outcome we do not know, but he did accept the Earl's offer of employment. When Gilby subsequently informed the authorities at Emmanuel College of his pending resignation, it caused an official vacancy to be posted for an elected fellow and Joseph applied, amongst others, when an open competition was duly advertised at the college. This action automatically made Gilby's current fellowship void. In the furtherance of Joseph's claim for elected fellowship, so far, so good.

However, a complication of some magnitude was about to befall this scheme for, just as the crux of the election for a new fellow was reached, the Earl of Huntingdon suddenly died. Poor Gilby in consequence therefore had no fellowship at Cambridge and effectively no job for Huntingdon either. Not surprisingly, Joseph felt very upset at the fate of his colleague, and probably not a little guilty too.

Joseph made an effort to extricate his friend and himself from this mess. He went to the college master and implored him to cancel the fellowship competition, reinstate Nathaniel Gilby and return to the *status quo*. However, there was an insurmountable problem. The College Master,

7

Lawrence Chadderton, would not entertain the annulment of the competition for Nathaniel Gilby had technically already been removed from the college, and could therefore under no circumstances be reinstated. The election for fellowship had to go ahead as originally planned. As Joseph states, following his attempt to intercede for Gilby "...
answer was made me, that the place was pronounced void".

From Joseph's later account of this sad turn of events we know that he and Nathaniel were mortified by the prevailing circumstances. It was the sort of predicament that friends would never elect to have to face. However, they were stuck with the Master's decision and the competition, already in full flow, had to run its course. Inevitably, to rub salt into the wounded Gilby, Joseph Hall won the contest, beating William Bradshaw, after what Joseph described as an *"exquisite"* examination. He was therefore duly elected to the position of fellow of Emmanuel College. However heavy his heart might have felt over this, Joseph accepted the elevated position, and Nathaniel Gilby effectively fades from the scene. One is left with feeling, yet again, that Joseph's path was smoothed before him. The next year, 1596, Joseph was awarded his Master of Arts Diploma.

First published work ... and a controversy

Joseph must have relished the thought of seeing himself in print for the first time. There is no doubting his intellectual capacity, for we know that Joseph had been a first rate student at Cambridge. A contemporary account claims that he *"passed all his degrees with great applause*, and now, in the 1590s, all his creative powers were being released. His first published work was a poem, (in a pastoral style) which was included within an elegy comprising items from several other writers to mark the death in 1595 of Anglican Theologian, William Whitaker, who was Master of St. John's College, Cambridge and said to be revered above all others by his contemporaries. Joseph's poem is almost one-hundred lines in length and expresses the great loss of one who was called the '*pride and ornament'* of his college. Two years later Joseph was published again, this time however things had changed for he did not share the title page with anyone else.

In 1597 Joseph Hall's first solo publication appeared. *Virgidemiarum* was an extensive work written in a satirical style following earlier Latin models by ancient writers such as Seneca, (circa 4 BC-65 AD). Within his lifetime

8

Joseph was to become known as the *'English Seneca'* - although he wouldn't have wished the comparison to be identical, for the Emperor Nero ordered Seneca to commit suicide! *Virgidemiarum* reprinted in English with its translated title reading *'A Harvest of Rods'*. The English edition provides evidence that Joseph Hall was the first to introduce several words into our language, including 'appurtenance' and 'galled'. Initial use of the word 'plagiary', and inventive terms such as 'hedge-creeping' (a clandestine act) and 'ding-thrift' (recklessness with money) are cited by *The Oxford English Dictionary* as Joseph's creations.

The subject matter of *Virgidemiarum*, together with its quasi-aggressive style, clearly set out to 'chastise' (hence the allusion to whipping rods) some contemporary authors who Joseph asserted were simply not up to it. Joseph could not abide their lax morals and the impurities in their use of the English language. Joseph had no truck with those he considered perhaps 'celebrity' authors merely furthering their careers. Joseph Hall's first 'book' was, in fact, a series of six volumes in total, published and bound in two sets of three, under the main title *Virgidemiarum*. The first three were grouped as *'Tooth-less Satyrs'* (1597) and the final three under the sub-heading of *'Biting Satyrs'* (1598). These writings have been described as 'socially trenchant'. It is worth stating that both volumes were very popular and reprinted in 1599 and 1602, although there is some doubt as to who actually commissioned the 1602 edition which quite probably was a

A beautiful title page dating from 1611, for the third and last volume of 'Epistles' written by Joseph Hall DD. It was published by Samuell Macham and sold at the Bull's Head, Saint Paul's Churchyard, London.

9

clandestine issue. Such unofficial editions by unscrupulous publishers were not that rare, for as long as they could evade the power of the Stationers' Company, a newly typeset edition could easily be issued which might well prove to be a good financial investment. 'Piracy' of someone's intellectual rights is by no means a modern phenomenon.

The initial prints of Joseph's first book in 1597/8 were probably of a rather limited quantity – perhaps no more than one hundred copies. At this time all print issues would have fallen within the strict terms of the Stationers' Court of 1587 which had stipulated that no books of more than 1,250 copies could be printed without the type being completely re-set. This ruling, prompted by the Church of England, had been brought into force in order to control the possible spread of subversive and blasphemous books. The Stationers' Company were also happy with this ruling as it was seen as an effective means of protecting the jobs of the printing trade's elite journeymen craftsmen.

In the prologue to his first tome Joseph claims, perhaps vainly, (but almost certainly with intentional provocation) to be the very first English satirist. He went further by including this taunting verse:

> *"I first adventure with foolhardy might,*
> *To tread the steps of perilous despite;*
> *I first adventure, follow me who list,*
> *And be the second English satirist".*

Flippantly tongue-in-cheek it caused a stir amongst a few writers who considered themselves already established satirical authors. Their bitingly terse reactions would seem however to clearly display that their abilities in this genre didn't necessarily mean that they had much of a general sense of humour to go with it! Particularly affronted by this young upstart from Cambridge was John Marston, (1576-1634) a self-acclaimed writer of satirical verse. Marston would hit back at Joseph in 1598 by publishing a fiercely condemnatory tract rejecting Joseph's claim of being the very first English satirist.

The dispute between Marston and Hall got progressively very bitter indeed. At one stage Marston actually accused Hall of pasting a satiric epigram into all of the copies of his own latest book *'The Metamophosis of Pigmalious*

Image' " . . . that came to the Stationers at Cambridge". Of course, living and working in Cambridge at this time would have given Joseph Hall a fairly easy opportunity (via a consenting third party perhaps) to intercept Marston's books and interfere with them. Although intriguing it's now doubtful we will ever know the truth in Marston's claim. However, I have a sneaky hunch that Joseph was probably guilty as charged. If nothing else, he was stirring up the 'establishment' and very definitely getting himself known.

In general, Hall's early writing style was considered by some observers to be a bit rough in its use of language, with rather obscure allusions, and, although wholesome in the main, there were passages considered to closely border on the scurrilous. However, when writing in verse he was considered to be both vigorous and witty.

The almost disparaging reference above to Joseph's 'obscure allusions' rather sadly misses the obvious. Of course his observations were indirect and devious, for this was a manifestation of his emerging skill in satirical writing. He was purposely teasing his adversaries by sharp observations of their traits; sufficient for them to know whom he was getting at, yet annoyingly opaque in his restraint of actually naming anyone. It was such an effectively deployed strategy that he was able to publicly annoy his targeted 'victims' whilst carefully avoiding litigation in response. *Private Eye* magazine is still flourishing today by generally successfully following this code of journalism – even to the point of shrewdly miss-spelling strategic names when necessary. If Joseph's protagonists had only taken the time to read his second set of books thoroughly they would have clearly seen this *modus operandi* declaration:

> *"Who dares accuse my frank satires of transparency? Whoever reads me has to rub his brow and puzzle over the intent of each line, scoring the margin with hundreds of blazing asterisks and interlinear squiggles."*

A flavour of Joseph's general moralistic style can be clearly seen in his biting satire on the theme of wilful infidelity and deceptive behaviour. Here he goes very near to the bone:

> *"Who wants out when wives hire snot-nosed youths for gigolos and feed them eggs and oysters as horse-breeders do their stallions at*

11

studding time? O goddess of childbirth, Lizzie gives her husband an heir after a dozen years of barren marriage – and bribes the midwife to swear the little bastard looks exactly like him!"

A burning topic

I doubt it caused Joseph any discomfort whatsoever at this time that he was considered self-opinionated and a little arrogant. He would have revelled in the thought that he was ruffling some pretty highly regarded and rather well-preened feathers. There were so many spats between all the above 'celebrities' that a decision was made at the very highest level to call a halt to all this published unpleasantness. The threatened action was draconian. On 1st June 1599 Dr John Whitgift, (1530-1604) the Archbishop of Canterbury, ordered that selected published satirical works by Hall, Marlowe, Marston, Thomas Nashe, (1567-1601) and others, numbering more than a dozen titles, were to be seized and burned at Stationer's Hall in London.

We have to remember that books were pretty scarce and meant a lot to their creators. They were expensive to produce and acquire. A public burning of these tomes would certainly be felt as an admonishment by the authors. It would also clearly demonstrate that there were limits of toleration in the hierarchy of the Church. However, it would appear that on reflection, and after further examination of the books impounded, only Joseph's books evaded the flames, for an edict was issued that his books *" . . . should be staide at the press"*. It is very likely that his clever writing had saved the day. His books were therefore reprieved and remained at the printer/publishers for sale and distribution. Joseph's guardian-angel had been busy yet again.

The emerging power of the press during the late 16th century should not be underestimated. The advent of printing from moveable type in England had emerged only a century before, coming to these shores from Germany and the Low Countries. In the 1580s many provincial cities and large towns were witnessing printing shops opening in their midst. Flemish craftsmen who came to this country a few years earlier in 1565 supplied much of this skill. By the time Joseph Hall was going into print, there were far more printers available than there were a few decades before, when basically only London, Oxford and Cambridge could have boasted of having

12

printers. However, authors were not confined to using English-based printers. In fact there was quite a flourishing trade importing printing and binding into this country from Europe at this time.

Perhaps some academics rather indulged themselves in this new era of publishing, for the content of these tit-for-tat publications was comparatively lightweight and ephemeral. We have to seriously question Joseph Hall's involvement in argumentative publishing. His enthusiasm for it rather showed up his immaturity. Perhaps he still needed his mother standing over him threatening to read him those pious Puritanical tracts at bedtime! His involvement in this rather futile, self-glorifying genre did come back to seriously taunt him only a handful of years later, as will be revealed in *Chapter Two.*

The only contemporary writer who mostly avoided Joseph's sharp quill was Edmund Spenser, (1552-1599) whose works he generally considered to be exemplary. Many commentators feel that Spenser's influence can be found in Joseph Hall's writings – especially in his poetic verse. Incidentally, when Spenser died Joseph was publicly indignant at the gross lack of respect shown to this great writer by the deplorable omission of any carved memorial stone being raised in his honour.

Joseph is likely to have been the culprit associated with a circulating scurrilous claim in the 1590s. In it, the anonymous writer asserted that some contemporary poets had such a warped regard of their self-promoted 'precious' writings that they would stoop so low as to have their works printed on shiny paper - then pasted up the sides of Mount Sion itself! One has to say it does have the ring of early Hall about it! Naturally, Joseph considered the prospect of any such act as wholly blasphemous.

The great desire to write never left Joseph. When one appreciates the sheer volume of his life's output, he must have been scratching away with his quill for several hours every day, when, that is, he had observed his lengthy daily prayerful meditation at day-break. One imagines he fretted like any other author over the printed accuracy of his works. This of itself of course brings forth the additional demand of making precious time available to endlessly proof-read and correct. As Joseph prepared to enter the next important phase of his life, he consciously decided to move on from satirical writings. Perhaps his sharp wit and intellect needed a new focus and a higher level of challenge. Joseph was now on the threshold of fulfilling the cherished dreams of his parents, and by entering the priesthood his character was set to mellow.

Drawn and engraved on a wooden printing block ca. 1642-43, shortly after his appointment to Norwich, (see *Chapter Four*) this is a delightfully reflective portrait of Joseph Hall. The use of the important 'pointing' (index) finger as a book-mark in the picture is interesting. It isn't just a casual part of the pose, for it adds gravitas to the portrait by clearly indicating the individual's literary skills and academic status, (plus a hint of "I wrote this book") as well as the importance he placed on showing the reader that there was perhaps a special tract therein which he held dear - as ought they. The original page bearing this fine effigy is an extremely fragile document housed in Norwich Cathedral Library. Handling and photographing this precious item was a very delicate task!
Photographed by kind permission of the Dean and Chapter, Norwich Cathedral.

CHAPTER TWO

Priesthood – marriage – children - Royal appointments

On 14th December 1600 Joseph was ordained into the priesthood at a ceremony in Colchester, Essex. He was first tempted into removing himself from Cambridge to Devon when he was offered the job of Master, at *Blundell's School* in Tiverton, which establishment is still thriving today with upwards of 800 students. However, even though this job had a very attractive remuneration attached to it, he decided not to accept it. Instead he stood aside to let his old college friend Hugh Cholmley take up the position. For so many years they had been side by side in all their educational endeavours, but now, for a while at least, came the parting of the ways as Hugh headed to the south west of England and Joseph, as it turned out, made for Suffolk. However, Devon would make a more powerful play for Joseph in due course.

Hawstead, Suffolk

Ann, Lady Drury approached Joseph during 1601 to test if he would be minded to take the living as Rector of All Saint's Parish Church in Hawstead, *(see page 24)* some three miles from Bury St. Edmunds, in Suffolk. I think it absolutely necessary to note here that many researchers have persistently and inaccurately made claim that Joseph was appointed to *Halstead*. It is a common theme of many books and other reference sources. The error has been freely perpetrated since the 19th century, but for all that doggedness it is still wrong – **Hawstead** in Suffolk is correct.

The Lady Anne was the wife of Sir Robert Drury, a wealthy man with influence, whose patronage Joseph no doubt originally thought would only assist his career. Joseph accepted the position on 2nd December 1601. In hindsight it was probably not the wisest move, for there was to be an on-going issue between both men regarding Joseph's salary. Sir Robert Drury, who no doubt Joseph respected for his position and status, was actually a rather mean-minded individual. The position of Rector at Hawstead had been instigated by Drury who justified the position on the basis that new tithes would be collected to cover the appointment. However, the truth of the matter turned out to be that Drury kept the largest portion of this income for himself, with only a pittance being passed to Joseph who, in a later autobiography, felt compelled to confide that he was *". . . forced to write books to buy books"*.

At age 27 Joseph was still a relatively young man, and, likely as not somewhat naive of the demands that might descend upon him in the outside world. Stuck in Suffolk it was also probably difficult for him to get the respect he maybe thought he was due on the back of his publishing ventures thus far. Even though there is no disputing that he was already well known to those in high places in the academic world, his fame as a rather gifted writer and published author might not have cut much ice here, where, in deepest rural Suffolk, he was almost certainly, generally speaking, relatively unknown.

Divine intervention?

Joseph was destined to learn rather quickly that life in a parish environment might not afford him the cosy shelter of Emmanuel College. I think it very likely that his somewhat qualified acceptance at Hawstead was a lot to do with his age. He might well have been considered quite a catch for the Drury's who would have moved in the right circles to read and appreciate his published works to date. However, there must have been many who simply thought him too young, (not to mention opinionated) for their church and parish. One particularly influential person in Joseph's new congregation seems to have 'had it in for him' from the start, for this belligerent character assailed him as soon as he arrived at Hawstead. Joseph had been used to holding his own in argument against some of the smartest brains in the land, but here, in this one abrasive character he was confronted by a wily and tenacious individual who was set on bringing him down a peg or three.

Maturity usually comes with an accompanying rounding experience of life, and Joseph was about to learn this lesson. Simply having his views opposed would not have struck Joseph as unreasonable, after all, in the past, he certainly hadn't been shy in robustly countering the opinions of others. No, this face-to-face corrosive attitude was new to him. He was vulnerable to it because of his inexperience, but not however unaware of its threat to his effective ministry. Just when he needed to make new friends and establish himself in doing God's work, he found instead that this rather evil character had not only seriously turned many parishioners against him, but his patron Sir Robert Drury too. This is what Joseph had to say about this rather nasty individual some years later when recalling this period in his life.

> *" . . . I found there a danger to the success of my ministry, a witty and bold atheist, one Mr Lilley, who by reason of his travails, and abilities of discourse and behaviour, had so deeply insinuated himself into my patron, Sir Robert Drury, that there was small hopes, during his entireness, [lifetime] for me to work any good upon that noble patron of mine, who, by the suggestion of this wicked detractor, was set off me before he knew me".*

Joseph admits to praying that this *"malicious hindrance might, by some act, be removed from blocking my ministry".* He declares that accordingly, and almost immediately after his prayerful beseeching, the problematical gentleman took himself hastily off to London, no doubt, (according to Joseph) to spread more mischief with Sir Robert Drury. However, divine intervention seems to have taken a hand here as the *"troublesome individual was swept away with the pestilence"* whilst in London, and perished.

'Mr Lilley' is almost certain to have been William Lyly, who was probably born at Hawstead in the early 1550s. It's worth looking into the background of this man as it helps to establish why Joseph was so unnerved by him. Lyly had been educated at Magdalen College, Oxford where he had been considered a witty livewire. He was a published author and playwright. There seems to have been a contemporary claim that William Shakespeare paraphrased a number of Lyly's original dramatic passages. He was a rather diminutive man and apparently much prone to taking tobacco! This habit would not have exactly endeared Lyly to Joseph who had earlier been on record as stating that those who so indulged, were *" . . . whiffing themselves away in Necotian Incense."* So do we see a character flaw emerging from Lyly that suggests he had a bit of a chip on his shoulder regarding the treatment of his precious writings? If so, perhaps literary jealousy lies at the heart of his hostility towards Joseph. Did Lyly consider Joseph an inferior upstart?

Lyly had seen duty in Paris between 1583 and 1590 as a staff member of the English Ambassador to France, Sir Edward Stafford. In the 1590s Lyly

17

married Ann, the eldest sister of the famous poet John Donne. On 11 April 1594 Ann Lyly and John Donne received the inheritance of their brother Henry who had died in 1593. A document still exists in which Ann Lyly and her husband William acknowledge receipt of the inheritance. From October 1596 to January 1598, William Lyly was with the English forces sent to Picardy to aid the King of France. After 1598 Lyly appears to have come back to live in Hawstead.

William Lyly had enjoyed a close relationship with the Drury family. He could always get the ear of Sir Robert, who himself was a favourite of Queen Elizabeth I. Lyly had acted as 'witness' on many legal documents on behalf of the Drury's. This responsibility would surely only have been entrusted to a favoured individual. Lyly was therefore certainly well connected and a much more experienced 'man of the world' when compared to Joseph, who was his junior by at least twenty-five years. Lyly could call on all that diplomatic service experience, not to mention the status he obviously enjoyed within the establishment at the time.

Being related through marriage to John Donne, Lyly could have seen this eminent poet's kinship as the perfect excuse to undermine Joseph's confidence and standing as a poet in his own right. Lyly knew where Joseph was vulnerable. Those early somewhat immature published satirical spats between Joseph and others were now seen as his Achilles heel, for Lyly would maliciously throw these works in Joseph's face as not being worthy of comparison with the works of the great genius John Donne – his brother-in-law, let alone himself. It looks as though Joseph only had to bear Lyly's ways from 1601-03, for on 16th August 1603 letters of administration were granted to Ann Lyly, *'relict of William Lyly, formerly of Hawstead in the County of Suffolk, deceased'.*

Any enmity betwixt Joseph and Lyly's kinsman John Donne was erased and forgotten by 1611 when Joseph, (now living in Essex) collaborated with Donne in a publishing venture. In that year Joseph was asked to contribute elegiac verse for the prefatory section of a printed memorial volume of poetry written by John Donne. This book was dedicated to Elizabeth Drury, the daughter of Joseph's then former patron, who had sadly just died at the tender age of fourteen. Owing to a strange twist of fate in 1619, both Joseph Hall and John Donne were set to be co-recipients of a rather stunning prize from the Netherlands. See *Chapter Three.*

On the second anniversary of the child's death in 1612, Donne wrote yet another book of memorial poems and again Joseph Hall provided some prefatory verse. In fact Joseph was more than a contributor to this volume for he oversaw its publication whilst Donne was abroad with Drury. Joseph, by now acquainted well enough with the demands of printers and their mysterious craft, accomplished the production of this memorial volume with some ease. He may have also felt he owed a degree of gratitude towards his former patron's wife, Ann – even if Joseph felt less obliged towards Drury himself owing to the man's meanness.

It is believed that Donne also composed the engraved epitaph on the young lady's tomb, whereon her effigy depicts her reclining - somewhat awkwardly on her left elbow. It can be found in the south sanctuary of All Saints Church, Hawstead, Suffolk, which church can probably claim to have more monuments and memorials than any other in that county. The child's death also ended the Drury's plans to announce her betrothal to Prince Henry, the eldest son of King James I.

Following Lyly's death in 1603, Joseph decided, after all, to stay in Hawstead and develop his calling there. Before anything else was to be achieved he felt he simply had to attend to the refurbishing of the dilapidated Vicarage, and turn it into a dwelling fit for his position. This action, (surely ringing of 'fresh start') would also have focussed the minds of his parishioners to the fact that he was here to stay. Perhaps it was time for his flock to desist from whatever prejudiced views they had been led to have of Joseph, and give the young man a chance. From this point onwards it is obvious that Joseph showed a degree more confidence in his ability to answer his calling, for, had his prayers not been heard and answered regarding the odious Lyly? Joseph was to remain at Hawstead until1608. The intervening years however were to prove anything but uneventful.

'Arranged' marriage?

When once the Vicarage refurbishment had been completed in 1603 Joseph, now a Bachelor of Divinity, was feeling the need for company and, at age 29, turned his thoughts towards having a wife. As ever, it seems, something out of the ordinary was about to be revealed to him on this matter, for Joseph recalls that on his way to a wedding-dinner, (how apt) on

Monday in Whitsun Week, and whilst in the company of the Reverend
Minister Mr Grandridge, the following extraordinary event occurred.

> "... I saw a comely and modest gentlewoman standing at the door
> of entry, and, inquiring of my worthy friend if he knew her, said
> yes, he knew her well and had already bespoken her for my wife.
> When I further demanded an account of that answer, he told me
> she was the daughter of a gentleman he much respected, Mr
> George Winniff [or, Whinniff] of Brettenham, [Suffolk] and
> he had already treated with her father about it, whom he found
> very apt to entertain it; advising me not to neglect the opportunity.
> At last, upon due prosecution, I happily prevailed; enjoying the
> comfortable society of that meet help for the space of forty-nine
> years".

Children – The Hall Dynasty

Joseph and Elizabeth married on 15 November 1603 at Bradfield St. Clare,
Suffolk. During their long partnership Elizabeth bore Joseph at least nine
children who reached an age beyond childhood. We know of no other
births. Joseph of course was also from a large family of perhaps twelve
siblings. Most researchers have attributed Joseph and Elizabeth with having
six children - five boys and a girl. However, I have taken the opportunity to
research further into their offspring and have to say the evidence for nine
children is compelling. The reader is directed to consult *Appendix B* for the
most complete listing of the Halls children, (and relating family matters)
yet compiled.

To Belgium - and a caution

Joseph could be forgiven for thinking that life at Hawstead was turning a
bit sweeter, even though he still could get no reconciliation with his measly
patron over his claim for an extra £10 per year. This wrangle was to
ultimately force Joseph to 'consider his position' at Hawstead. For the
meanwhile he got on with his ministry there as best he could. Married life
was not disappointing him for surely we see a renewed literary appetite in
the publication of several notable and highly regarded books during the
next few years. *'Meditations and Vowes'*, (1605); *'Heaven upon Earth'*,
(1606), and *'The Arte of Divine Meditation'*, (1606) attest to this. In
addition to these volumes he also wrote a number of essays that were

20

strongly influenced by his own Christian morality. These works included his *'Epistles'*, (1606-8), and *'Characters of Vertues and Vices'* (1608).

In 1605 Joseph was chosen to accompany Sir Edmund Bacon, (Lady Drury's brother) on an Embassy to Spa in Belgium. The purpose of this journey was to observe and learn first hand about the Roman Catholic religion. On this mission, (which Joseph enigmatically later referred to as being *'secret')* he was apparently- perhaps appropriately- dressed as a layman. He rather astonished the Roman Catholic priests and Jesuits he met with his great understanding of theological matters. They also marvelled at his superior knowledge of Latin. However, Joseph had not yet developed the knack of moderacy and tact for he managed to get himself rather embroiled in deep arguments about so-called modern miracles.

The person most offended was one William Baldwin, a Jesuit and Vice-Prefect of the English Mission to Brussels. Joseph also seems to have delighted in taunting an elderly Jesuit, Father Costerus who was known to be more testy than subtle in his own arguments. In perhaps a volatile atmosphere Joseph arrogantly dismissed all the arguments of the elderly Father by virtue of his superior academic prowess. This did not go down well, and, after official complaints about his brusque behaviour, Sir Edmund Bacon was forced to take Joseph to one side and issue him with what was effectively a gagging order, forbidding him from entering into any further contentious discussions. However, notwithstanding this episode, the assignment had certainly at the very least got Joseph noticed.

Meditation- a new perspective

The appearance of *'Mundus alter at idem'*, (A New World Yet the Same) printed in Latin in Frankfurt' (2 volumes, 1605) was quite an achievement for someone who had been abroad for part of the year. This satirical-cum-slightly-bawdy book was so popular that it reprinted again in Frankfurt in 1607 and again, in English this time in London in 1608, (2 volumes) using as its title *"The discovery of a New World"*. The book is full of strange characters set in exotic make-believe places. Hall's vivid imagination for instance has women living in *'Aphrodisia'* and *'Hermaphroditica'* and fools dwelling in *'Moronia'*. The scope of the book is thus pretty obvious! There is interesting speculation that *Mundus alter at idem*, was the inspiration behind Jonathan Swift's famous novel *Gulliver's Travels,*

21

published in 1726. The whole success of *Mundus* is the more extraordinary for the fact that it was seemingly written whilst Joseph was a student at college then released for publication by Emmanuel College in Cambridge – some years later without the author's consent.

The appearance of *'The Arte of Divine Meditation'* (1606) has made many commentators take the view that this phase of Joseph's published output was beginning to greatly influence the development of English religious verse. It is now thought likely that this book was probably inspired during Joseph's experiences the previous year on the continent. Others before him had promoted the wisdom of contemplative meditation, and often recommended it be sought in the atmosphere of silence and solitude. We know from his own autobiographical comments that Joseph spent time every day, often from the earliest hours after waking, preparing himself in this way for the day ahead.

The writings of Thomas á Kempis, (ca. 1380-1471) may well have been the model Joseph had in mind when he turned his fertile brain to meditative tracts. Joseph lived over a century after á Kempis and brought his own fresh insights and mental energies to the practice of contemplative prayer. In essence Joseph put forward three suggestions to his readers whereby they might more easily find new ways of disciplining themselves to benefit from silent, prayerful reflection. He felt that one could do more than simply kneel down with a bible or prayer book in the hope that something useful might be found. Joseph extolled the merits of preparing oneself first so as to be receptive to meditative thoughts, then the levels of reactive inspiration could well be triggered by:

a) external stimulus: such as birdsong or the starry heavens.
b) rational thought: such as thinking about inspirational biblical subjects such as the parables or miracles of Jesus.
c) self-examination: this one likely to involve searching one's soul.

Joseph's meditative instruction was therefore not unique nor indeed was it particularly historically radical. However it was coming from the pen of a respected theologian who was reaching a readership that was keen to try something we can fairly say was at the least a new vision in that era. Many would come to the conclusion, (even in his lifetime) that Joseph Hall's *Meditations* were the best loved and most profound of all his writings.

Lady Ann Drury's 'Panels'

Joseph's patron's wife, the Lady Ann Drury may well have agreed with this statement. We know that she took her own private meditations very seriously. The proof of this is revealed in the contents of a very small private closet reserved for her devotions at Hawstead Place, her country home. The somewhat surprising fact is that she had this space decorated with forty-one painted wooden panels depicting a varied sequence of scenes. The workmanship is considered to be very accomplished and there is a view that she may well have painted them herself. These very interesting plaques can today be found within the Ipswich Museums Service at Christchurch Mansion, near the centre of Ipswich, Suffolk, where they are on display in a closet above the porch. Experts have dated these objects to the early 17th century – about 1615 at the latest.

Space does not allow for a complete listing of the varied subject matter contained in the full collection. Suffice it to say that they include the following: A camel wading through dirty water; a flying eagle with an elephant in its talons; a man endeavouring to light a candle using a glow-worm; a mermaid with comb and glass and another showing a full bucket of water at the top of a well shaft.

It is believed that Lady Ann Drury may well have used all her panels as allegorical inspirations towards meditation. In quiet contemplation the evocative subject matter of these paintings could be pondered upon. If they were so used it is quite likely she was simply following the advice she had no doubt come by via Joseph Hall's sermons in her parish church, or indeed from reading his published *Meditations*, as mentioned above.

Royal Command Performance

Following the success of his *'Arte of Meditation'* in 1606 Joseph published a very important sequel with his *'One Hundred Meditation's* (ca. 1607). This collection is commonly considered by his later biographers to be *the* book that marked a turning point in his writing career. He came to excel when writing in this style. His meditations soon came to be considered with higher regard than his sermons. The young Henry, Prince of Wales, (eldest son of King James I and named after Henry Lord Darnley and Henry VII) read a copy of the 1606 *Meditations* and requested that he be able to hear the author preach. Joseph must have been both delighted, yet somewhat wary of receiving an order to appear before royalty. Obviously the Royal Command Performance of its day! Nevertheless he duly obeyed and preached before the young prince at Richmond Palace in 1606. He later recalled, (rather self-deprecatingly) that his royal sermon was *" . . . not so well given as received"*.

Joseph had obviously impressed the young prince for in 1608 he was appointed as one of many personal chaplains to the young royal and technically remained so until New Year's Day 1613. Nearly fifty of Joseph's sermons are extant covering the years 1608-1643. However, during my research I found reference to another – probably his last - delivered on 1st July 1655. An excerpt is printed in *Chapter Five*.

In the early summer of 1607 Joseph determined to press, yet again, for the full salary he was due at Hawstead. The dispute was over an extra £10 per annum. He travelled to London to confront Sir Robert Drury at his home in Drury Lane, where, almost inevitably, he was badly received by his patron who discourteously admonished Joseph for his audacity in approaching him over the matter. Joseph left his company forthwith, fully resolved to leave Hawstead as soon as possible.

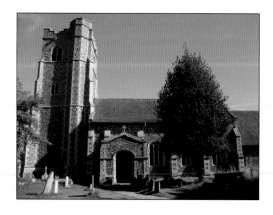

All Saint's Parish Church, Hawstead, Suffolk

CHAPTER THREE

Waltham Abbey - The Netherlands – Exeter -
The 'Smectymnuus' affair

As ever, it seems, bountiful providence was set to cheer Joseph for, almost immediately, he received a summons to meet Baron Edward Denny of Waltham who, having read some of Joseph's works on meditation, and having heard of his great preaching abilities, was minded to appoint him as chaplain to his household and as Rector at Waltham Abbey. On hearing this news, Joseph's current patron offered to accede to Joseph's previous claim. Joseph resolutely refused to entertain Drury's belated offer and, *". . . returned home, happy in a new master, and in a new patron, betwixt whom I divided myself and my labours with much comfort and no less acceptation."*

Probably by late summer in 1608 Joseph and family had moved to the parish of Waltham-Holy-Cross, Essex, with his church being Waltham Abbey. Lord Denny, (later to become Edward Denny, 1st Baron Rose, 1st Earl of Norwich in1626) had appointed Joseph to a church of great historical interest, for it had originally been founded by King Harold and dedicated to the Holy Cross. Much damage had been done at the Reformation with the pulling down of the chancel and choir. A new tower, (obvious from the fine picture above) had been erected.

In 1608 Joseph was asked by the young prince Henry to become his personal chaplain. This offer of promotion would mean almost constant attendance at Court. Joseph considered himself unworthy for the post and *" . . . did modestly put it off, and held close to my Waltham, where, in a constant course, I preached a long time, as I had done also at Hawstead before, thrice in the week . . . whereof I . . . penned every word in the same order, wherein I hoped to deliver it."*

1608 was a busy year for Joseph for shortly after his arrival at Waltham he published a significant literary work on biblical characters. A shrewd move saw Joseph dedicate this work, (and an *'Epistle – see page 103*) to his new patron, Edward, Lord Denny, Baron of Waltham. Joseph courted controversy again when his anti-Catholic volume, *'The Penance of Rome'* *(*1609) was published. The Vatican was swift in its condemnation of this work wherein the writer maintained that Roman Catholicism was *". . . a true visible Church in respect of outward profession of Christianity"* but *" an heriticall Apostaticall, Anti-christian synagogue in respect of doctrine and practice".*

Joseph Hall defends the Church

Since the 1580s a rather radical group of individuals had taken a stand for independent thought as regards religious adherence in England. They berated the stuffy, formal nature of the Church of England, whose ceremonial and garb they considered pompous. The extremists were collectively known as 'The Brownists', so named after their 'founder' Robert Browne, (1550-1633) who was born in Tolethorpe, Rutland, of wealthy parents well-connected with the all-powerful Cecil family. Browne showed early promise at Cambridge University 1570-73 receiving a BA in 1572. It was here that he and a Norwich man, Robert Harrison, (ca1540-85) became radicalised by the Puritan theologian Thomas Cartwright, (1535-1603). In 1580 Browne travelled to Norwich and there founded a separatist congregation, which was the embryo of what came to be the Independent and Congregationalist movements.

Brown published *'A Booke Which Sheweth the Life and Manners of All True Christians'* (1582) and *'A Treatise of Reformation Without Tarying for Anie'*(1582). In the latter document Browne declared his ideal church would not raise tithes for there would be no professional clergy as such. Only voluntary financial offerings would be asked for and such a body would elect its own preachers. Co-operation with other religious groups would be purely voluntary. In 1610 Joseph Hall wrote in terse terms to defend the Church of England against the assertions of the Brownist's. Joseph's pithy admonishment obviously stung the Brownist's for they retaliated by publishing a pamphlet titled *"An Answer to a Censorius Epistle".* In response Joseph attacked with a long terse document entitled *"A Common Apology* [defence] *against the Brownists."*. To this there was no answer. Joseph Hall's resolve had therefore neutralised any threat the

Brownists could have been to the Church. Brown apparently died in Northampton gaol in 1630, totally decrepit, aged 81.

Sleep well, sweet prince

By 1612 Joseph had attained his Doctor of Divinity diploma and that very year he dedicated the first part of his *Contemplations* to the young Prince Henry – even though the full work was not to be finished until after 1627 in Exeter. However, much sadness was set to attach itself to this early volume for it was to be the very last of his works that the young royal would read, for he died suddenly on 6th November 1612. Joseph attended the funeral and went on to preach a comforting sermon to the royal household on New Year's Day 1613. It was a solemn occasion and Joseph spoke with great tenderness. He would greatly miss his young charge and wrote two elegies to mark his passing. On the night of the prince's death an extraordinary vision was seen by many in the vicinity of St. James' Palace in London – a rainbow appeared after dark. Joseph wrote in his second elegy that the astonishing spectacle had been sent to convey comfort to those in grief and was an assurance that Henry had received a better crown. Later that year Joseph came to prominence by delivering a very flattering sermon, (also issued as a printed pamphlet) celebrating the tenth anniversary of the accession to the throne of England by King James I.

In 1616, whilst on yet another European mission, (this time in France with Viscount Doncaster) news broke of Joseph's appointment as Dean of Worcester. Although he was expecting a preferment at some point his selection for this post was surprisingly not made known to him before leaving England. Joseph was to be taken rather ill whilst on this excursion, (his self-diagnosis being *'Diarrohoea Bilosa'*) and the attack was so severe that he only got back to England with the greatest of difficulty. The welcome news of his promotion must have cheered him.

The following year, (1617) Dean Hall, with William Laud, Dean of Gloucester, and others, travelled to Scotland to personally assist King James I in his intention to force the *Five Articles of Perth* on the Scottish nation. The King wished for the Scots to follow certain practises in their own worship, which were common in usage amongst those in the English Episcopalian Church. The articles were: 1. Kneeling during the Communion. 2. Private Baptisms. 3. Private Communion for those sick or infirm. 4. Confirmation by a Bishop and 5. Observance of all Holy Days. After a full year deliberating on the matter, the Scots reluctantly accepted the *Articles of Perth* in 1618. However, it was not until 1621 that the Scottish Parliament actually ratified its agreement to these rules. It was obviously an on-going aggravation for them because in 1690 they were swift to repeal this imposition.

A Royal assignment

In 1618 Dean Hall was to go abroad again, this time as a member of the English Delegation to the 'Synod of Dort' held in the Council Chamber of the *Doel* in Dordrecht, Holland. The term 'Dort' was a colloquial invention used over many years by English delegates. On this occasion the Synod is believed to have been in continuous session from about 13th November 1618 through to the 9th May 1619.

King James personally vetted and selected the five delegates to represent his kingdom. Just to make sure that his team were united and focussed, the King called them all together at Newmarket in 1618, (one of his favourite equine retreats) and advised them to practise their Latin and agree among themselves to attack if necessary any *"hellish doctrines"* which might arise. However, he generally urged them towards moderacy in all other matters. The original delegates were: *Bishop George Carleton* of Llandaff, *Dean Joseph Hall* of Worcester, *John Davenant* – Professor of Divinity and Theology at Cambridge and *Dr Samuel Ward* – Master of Sydney Sussex College, Cambridge.

At a later date *Dr Thomas Goad* was engaged to replace Joseph Hall, owing again to the latter's indisposition and *Dr Walter Bancanquall* attended for the Scottish Church. In all, the English Delegation eventually reached their allotted total of five delegates. Although the Synod of Dort was very much an international affair, the English delegates were held in high regard and their contributions to debate were eagerly awaited. The attendance of the English members, (collectively allowed a princely £10 per day subsistence) was entirely funded by the hosting Doel Council. The other attendees at Dort came from the Palatinate, Hesse, Switzerland, Geneva, Bremen and Emden. Dutch and Walloon divines also attended. On special occasions members of the public were allowed admission. I have

28

seen one engraving of the Synod in council that shows one casual gentleman observer with a small dog on a lead!

The Synod was governed by five professors from the hosting university and associated with them were twenty-one lay elders. In all, about one-hundred and twenty-five persons attended the daily sessions. This Synod had been called to look into and advise upon the legitimacy of the controversial 'Arminian' faction within the Dutch Church. Those so called were followers of Jacobus Arminius, (1560-1609) and rather than adopt the name of their leader they themselves choose instead to be known as the 'Remonstrants'. This issue had grown over the previous decade and centred on the Calvinist doctrine of predestination - that is to say that God predetermines all things for all people without selectivity. It also sought to define a true reconciliation of the relationship between civil and ecclesiastical authority.

Arminianism was a school of belief within the Calvinist Church that in fact had direct links with the foundation in England of the Baptist, Methodist and Unitarian Churches. In 1610, the year after their leader died, the Arminians presented the Dutch Church, (The States of Holland) with a five-point 'Remonstrance' whereby they rejected several core beliefs of Calvinist theology. This is what led to the Dutch Church deciding they needed to critically analyse the claims of the Remonstrants once and for all.

Their quest, via the Synod of Dort, was to determine if they could accommodate the Remonstrants' doctrine – or declare against it and thereby condemn and effectively ban Arminianism from the Dutch Church. The Remonstrants' main points of doctrinal disagreement with the Calvinist Dutch Church were:

a) Divine predestination is conditional – not absolute.
b) The atonement is universal as God died for all – not just for the specially 'chosen ones'.
c) Man is utterly depraved and not capable of saving himself.
d) Mankind has the free-will to deny God.
e) A believer in God's grace can deny Satan and be protected by God who will not allow the evil one to take them.

Joseph addresses Synod twice

We know Joseph Hall made a keynote speech to Synod on 29th November 1618. The story goes that, as the Remonstrants had not yet shown up at Synod the hosts implored the English delegation to nominate someone to address the general council in Latin. All of Joseph's compatriots had convenient excuses as to why they could not accede to this wish, but Joseph, grasping the opportunity with relish, saved any English blushes. He took as his text "Be not righteous over much; neither make thyself over wise". This quotation comes from the book of Ecclesiastes 7:16 which verse also ends with "why shouldest thou destroy thyself?" Having scanned through this highly acclaimed sermon a conservative estimate would suggest it would have taken forty-five minutes to deliver to Synod.

During this speech Joseph delicately wove references to the similarities between King Solomon and his monarch and sponsor, King James I of England who was also considered to be a very wise and learned ruler. King James is known to have thought of himself as a prince among holy rulers. Joseph, ever shrewd when it came to furthering his own aims when compatible with political sensitivities, had this address published for sale in Latin, (as delivered) in 1619 and then in English in 1621. Both items were printed in Geneva.

Joseph was quite keen to publish and sell miscellaneous personal papers from time to time. In due course he was even to have his speeches in the House of Lords printed and published. However infrequently these sundry publications might have appeared, they would nevertheless have promoted interest in his views as well as generate him useful income.

Joseph Hall was obviously not a robust traveller, (or his safe dietary needs were compromised) for in an unfortunate repeat of his 1616 journey to France, he was struck down with sickness during Synod. It was very likely a re-occurrence of what he described his illness had been those two years earlier – *'Diarrohoea Bilosa'*. Although it was a serious setback for Joseph he nevertheless delivered a major second address to Synod on 7th January 1619. It also had been specially prepared in Latin and, somewhat against the odds, he preached convincingly well by all accounts. His theme was that of moderation and mutual charity. The sound of enthusiastic applause round the chamber at its conclusion would have elated the ailing Joseph.

Early exit from Synod and grim news

On 8th January 1619, (immediately following this rather stressful preaching ordeal) Joseph begged permission to retire from the rest of the proceedings. He removed himself thence to The Hague, where he was tenderly nursed in the house of the English Ambassador, Dudley Carleton. Eventually, and with much distress, Joseph finally made it back to England and his home in Waltham. Joseph's illness had been so severe that rumours of his death had twice been in circulation. However, on 25th April 1619 Joseph wrote to Ambassador Carleton in The Hague that he was alive and making a slow recovery. It must have been shortly after his arrival back in Waltham that he received some truly awful news from Holland.

The Synod of Dort had irrevocably rejected the Remonstrants' demands and a select group of divines, (including Bishop George Carleton of Llandaff from the English delegation) met to invoke the Synod's view and issued a *Canon of Dort,* which effectively expelled the Arminian's from the Dutch Church. But this was not the worst of it.

Unknown to the English delegation, and prior to the opening of the Dort Synod, in a bid to quell any outward public manifestations of opposition to the Dutch Church's authority, a well known proponent of Arminianism, Johan van Oldenbarnveldt, had been rounded up, arrested and imprisoned on 29th August 1618 – nearly three months before the Synod first convened on 13th November of that year. Almost directly after Synod closed on 9th May 1619, (with its declaration of the expulsion of his sect) Johan van Oldenbarnveldt was beheaded only four days later on 13th May. With this bloody action the Dutch Church sent unequivocal and chilling notice to the Remonstrants.

When news of this grisly deed eventually reached Joseph, one can imagine that this fair-minded and moderate man who had just preached tolerance to the Doel at Dort must have been appalled. We could easily forgive him for feeling that his very attendance at Dort had seriously compromised and demeaned his high public standing. In mitigation he could of course ponder on the fact that his indisposition and early exit from the proceedings went some way towards protecting his untarnished character. Yes, he had been there – but not at the sickening end.

A prestigious award

Whatever uneasiness Joseph felt about the utter sadness surrounding the end of the Dort Synod he was soon to receive some amazingly good personal news. The Doel had decided to award him the highest accolade - their exceptionally rare gold medal. As Joseph later recounted, he was presented with a " . . . *rich Medall of Gold"* showing *"the portraicture of the Synod"*

This sumptuous medal, weighing 4ozs Troy, (one third of a pound) of pure 24 carat gold and measuring some 57mm in diameter, was probably delivered to him in Waltham, England. It was a very generous mark of the Synod's utter respect for his excellent addresses to them. It is hard to believe that its receipt by Joseph was anything other than an immensely gratifying surprise. We can only imagine his utter delight in gazing for the

first time on this fabulous object. I can say I certainly felt the same emotion when I was allowed to closely inspect, and even handle the medal at the Fitzwilliam Museum in Cambridge on 19th April 2011. The creation of this special token was the talented work of the designer Daniel Heinsius and the engraver Willem van Biljaar who was actually responsible for striking the series of Dort medals. Close scrutiny of the medal was rewarding for it contains some remarkable details.

On the obverse, *(pictured left)* the date of 1619 is seen split between the bottom left and right sectors of the detailed view inside the Synod chamber. The medal bears this date as it represents the year in which the synod concluded, (on 9th May) having convened and commenced on 25th November 1618. During the protractive synodical investigations the full councils met on at least 154 occasions – some accounts register as many as180 sittings! Close inspection of this side of the medal also revealed a depiction, (albeit in a rather stylised form) of the five actual members of the English Delegation sent to Dort by King James I, and named at the start of this chapter. One has to look to the right of the main central table, (as viewing the medal) where five tiny people can just about be observed on two seats of two, with a single seated person in front. Could the lone-seated delegate depicted here possibly be Joseph one wonders?.

A rather pedantic-looking touch by the engraver, (Willem van Biljaar) quite clearly shows empty seats to the immediate left, (*right* as viewed) of the English representatives. The engraver was following orders here for the vacant seats represent the fact that King Louis XIII of France refused to let a delegation of Huguenots attend the Synod. The design is therefore historically accurate. This side of the medal also contains the legend ASSERTA + RELIGIONE (Religion maintained) around the facing rim.

On the reverse side of the medal, *(left)* is a representation of an almost insurmountable rocky peak. In four separate sectors the four ill winds are blowing fiercely onto the rock face from broody, billowing clouds. Close scrutiny of the medal at the Fitzwilliam Museum, Cambridge, revealed that there are two miniscule climbers, valiantly attempting to reach the safe haven of the temple atop the mountain. Radiant sunbeams shine down onto the crown of the peak, which is Mount Sion itself. The climbers represent all those true souls who would pit their spiritual strength against any odds to remain firm in their faith and biblical beliefs, whilst also valiantly searching out the truth – undaunted by the difficulty of the task. Above the radiating sunbeams is the Lord himself, represented here by the Hebrew Tetragrammaton – YHWH – YAHWEH, (Jehovah). The facing outer rim contains the legend ERVNT + VT + MONS + SION + (They shall be even as the Mount Sion) with the date 1619 in arcane Roman numerals. The award of this astonishing medal would allow Joseph to bask in its prestigious status for the rest of his life, for, after its gift he is hardly ever shown in printed wood block engravings without it being seen pinned to his rochet, (surplice). However, in practice, it could not have easily been so worn for it is far too heavy. It must have been pinned right through to an under cassock for any degree of tidy stability. *(See page 36)*. All the English Delegates in 1618/19 received a silver version of the gold Dort medal with very attractive gold chains attached. However, the only gold medal awarded to a Dort delegate was that presented to Joseph Hall. We now know that Willem van Biljaar struck another identical medal in gold in 1619 and this item, for a different reason, also finished up in the hands of another Englishman. The famous English poet and essayist John Donne, whose path Joseph had crossed some years ago at Hawstead, (see *Chapter Two*) was also to receive a Dort medal in gold even though he had not attended the Synod. Donne was Dean of St. Paul's Cathedral, London, at this time. In December 1619 he had been appointed as chaplain to an embassy sent by King James I to the Netherlands under the leadership of Viscount Doncaster. Their mission was to diplomatically support the Dutch Protestant Church without upsetting the Calvinists who were the nationally approved church. Donne, a very astute and politically aware speaker, apparently delivered a brilliant sermon at a special service held in The Hague, wherein he advocated for religious tolerance and moderacy betwixt the Dutch Church and Protestantism.

It is not known conclusively if the Dutch Church was officially represented at this potentially delicate occasion but, if they were not, then someone must have reported to them the mastery of Donne's sensitive language. Awarding a gold Dort medal to Donne was a very generous token of their esteem. The recipient must surely have been delighted – and surprised. Perhaps the Dutch Church also weighed up the fact that this award would play well as a political gesture towards the Church in England.

I can't resist commenting that those English delegates who had sat through perhaps 180 successive synodical committee meetings - for which they 'only' received a silver medal, (albeit with a gold chain attached) - might have thought that the gold version awarded to Donne for a single sermon, (however brilliant) was more easily come by!

The medal today

A gold version of a Dort medal is seen rather rarely today. Silver versions have been known to fetch anything from £950 to £1400 each during auctions since 2007. One high class London salesroom, when pressed for a

34

current gold medal value, ventured to suggest that a price of £15-20,000 could be realised in auction, if one in excellent condition was to come onto the market. The Fitzwilliam's Dort medal is in a very good state of preservation, without any appreciably serious signs of wear. Old Joseph must have handled it very carefully as well as lovingly all those years ago. Wouldn't he be staggered to know his medal today is probably worth several tens of thousands of pounds - thanks to the current high price of gold?

In his will, detailed in *Chapter Five*, Joseph's clear wish was to declare that this much loved and treasured token must go to the eldest male child of one of his surviving sons. At the time of drawing up his will, (1654 – with a codicil added in 1655, a year before his death) Joseph remarked that only one son had any children - and they were both girls. If matters did not change he instructed that the medal should be given to his grandson Joseph Weld, the son of his surviving second daughter, Ann. In the outturn this did not quite come to pass as he had wished.

According to the excellent records maintained at Emmanuel College Cambridge, (and my indebtedness to Dr Amanda Goode in their Archive Department is significant) the medal passed directly to Joseph Hall's surviving daughter Ann, (Weld) who we might well suppose kept charge of the medal until young Joseph, (probably five in 1656) reached his majority. However, his mother, (Ann) left this precious item to her eldest daughter Mary, born 1645. It did not pass to young Joseph. Mary married a William Starkey and had a daughter - another Mary, who inherited the medal. She in turn married John Jermy and they had a son, William Jermy, who was bequeathed the medal from his mother. William Jermy's will was drawn up on 12 December 1751 and within its directions was his wish that the medal, (originally presented to his great, great, great grandfather) was to be donated to Joseph Hall's old college, Emmanuel, in Cambridge. William died the next year, (1752) when Emmanuel duly inherited the prized medal. I am informed that a miniature of Bishop Joseph Hall was also received from William Jermy at this time. Sadly it has gone missing. It is quite likely that this portrait would have been the 'master image' on which a number of wood-cuts of Joseph were based.

Why Joseph Weld was never given custody of the medal is a mystery, for he lived into his 60s having achieved high public office as Sergeant at law and Recorder for Bury St. Edmunds, Suffolk. He was also the town's MP 1709-12. He died 18th January 1712, (1711) in London aged 61. He lies in the floor of the crypt at St Mary's church Bury St Edmunds where the stone records his death as 1711. He was educated at Norwich School by 1665 and at Christ's College, Cambridge 1668. Therefore there seem to be no grounds regarding his incapacity to inherit his grandfather's prized possession. Emmanuel College kept the medal from 1752 until 1950 when it was offered on perpetual loan to the Fitzwilliam Museum, Cambridge, (together with over three-dozen other coins and medals) in a letter from the college Bursar, Robert Gardner, dated 14th December 1950.

The Fitzwilliam Museum agreed to have the items deposited with them and formally logged their arrival (including Joseph Hall's Dort Medal) in their Coins and Medals Department on 18th December 1950. I am very indebted to the Fitzwilliam Museum's Coins and Medals Department – and to Dr Martin Allen in particular - for all his willing and helpful assistance during my researches into the Dort medal and other associated topics. (See also details of Joseph Hall's will in *Chapter Five*).

Depicted here we see bishop Joseph Hall of Norwich in an engraving that can be dated to ca. 1654. It has been specially coloured for use on the cover of this book. (See *Title Page* for original print). It is possibly the last portrait of him. In all likelihood it shows him sitting at his writing desk in his study at Heigham Palace. The Dort medal is prominent on his breast, clearly communicating to the viewer of this fine printed wood-block image exactly what Joseph intended – his very great pride in being seen wearing it! On some prints the engraver has incorporated the word 'Synod' into the medal detail. Even though this word is not actually on the medal itself, *(see image page 32)* I daresay Joseph was tolerant of this artistic licence, for he was more than happy for his readers to know of the medal's prestigious provenance.

Gloucester refused – Exeter preferred

In 1624 Dean Hall, perhaps surprisingly, refused to accept his promotion to the Bishopric of Gloucester - *"with much humble deprecation"*. It's difficult to know for certain why Joseph refused for King James I was obviously intent on rewarding him for notable public service. Joseph was not simply a very able and learned churchman, for he had on occasion achieved some renown in the church courts where he had acted for clients facing litigation. It is likely that it was just such an involvement with ecclesiastical law in that part of the country which made him decide against Gloucester, for investigation into this matter has revealed the following.

Joseph had been asked to intervene in a law suite between Samuel Burton, (a kinsman who was then Archdeacon of Gloucester) and Sir Walter Leveson. In essence, Joseph had successfully seen Sir Walter Leveson found guilty of misappropriating monies from the church in Wolverhampton. This successful outcome had been fought in a Gloucestershire court. It is likely that a shrewd Joseph thought it best to steer clear of this region where he just might now have influential enemies in high places.

Joseph was now frequently moving in privileged places. In September of the same year, (1624) he preached in the presence of King James I. A copy of this sermon still survives and study reveals a rather stunning fact, over and above the merit of the content. At a conservative estimate I judge this oration must have taken at least fifty-five minutes to deliver! Long sermons were then of course considered to be a mark of the preacher's depth of faith and scholarship. During the Commonwealth inquisitions, priests who only gave thirty-minute sermons were held to be rather suspicious and considered lax in their duty. However, if we are looking for preaching duration records then surely Laurence Chadderton, the first, (and Joseph's) Master appointed at Emmanuel College in 1583 has to be the prime contender, for on one occasion he preached for two hours – then, offering to stop fearing likely audience fatigue, was exhorted by all gathered there with a chorus of *"For God's sake, Sir, go on, we beg you – go on!"* . . . and he did - for yet another hour! Chaderton was also a favourite of James I who selected him, amongst others, to translate earlier bibles to produce the King James Bible in 1611.

On 5th November1627 Joseph consented to his election as Bishop of Exeter, and he was duly consecrated there on 23rd December. By all accounts the fourteen years he spent in Exeter were, on the whole, fairly happy ones. Within two years of his appointment his second daughter Elizabeth, then aged nineteen was married to Dr William Peterson, (the Dean of Exeter) on 28th July 1629. It was a busy month for Dr Peterson who had been confirmed as Dean of Exeter only ten days before on 18th July 1629. The Halls must have considered their daughter had married well. Sadly, this union did not bear children and Elizabeth was to die on 8th July 1651 aged only forty-one. Dr Peterson held the post of Dean at Exeter until his death sometime late in the year 1661, for he was succeeded by Dr Seth Ward on 26th December that year. On paper, his tenure as Dean of Exeter extended to more than thirty years – a very considerable length of time. However, part of this occupancy may well have included those years when generally the activities of cathedral Chapters were suspended by Parliament during the Commonwealth period ca. 1641-59.

Suspicions and spies

Whilst in Exeter, Bishop Hall became somewhat renowned for his persistent stance of moderacy towards Catholics. He maintained that it was not good enough to dogmatically refute Roman Catholic doctrines out of hand. He was also under the impression that the clergy in his diocese fully supported him in this view. However, it is likely that he was being somewhat 'economical with the truth' here, as it is widely thought now that he was probably referring to the general support of his *governance* of the church in his diocese, and not the *doctrine*. He thought that *" . . . Puritanism was purely a refractory opposition to the ceremonies, rites and customes of the church"*.

By now the monarchy had passed to Charles I, and the King, (married to a Catholic princess) not surprisingly largely agreed with Bishop Hall's view. However, William Laud, (then Bishop of London) and others were deeply sceptical of what were seen as Joseph's lenient views. Laud went to the extreme of sending spies into Exeter to watch and note Bishop Hall's every move and public utterance, especially if it seemed to lend succour to the Papist's view, or be in any other way 'suspicious.' We could say that Joseph was sometimes tolerant towards Catholicism as indeed he was also at least sympathetic towards the Puritan movement in his early career –

which is hardly surprising when one considers his eight years at Emmanuel College Cambridge where he had been immersed in the influence of that establishment's Puritan ideals.

Joseph Hall now had powerful enemies in high places. His future would be attended by suspicion, and, should he step outside the rules of the elite church authorities, he could be certain of repercussions. Under these circumstances even an honourable and fair man like Joseph Hall would not escape unwarranted criticism. It must have been a trying time for Joseph for even though he had a powerful ally in the King, Bishop Laud saw to it that Joseph's career was effectively blocked at Exeter.

For a while, Joseph seemingly had adversaries on every side of the religious divide. In an effort to come to his defence and calm things down a bit, his old school and college friend, Hugh Cholmley, (now Joseph's Chaplain) waded in with his own book titled *"The State of the now-Romane Church"* (1629). It probably didn't calm many of Joseph's detractors to read that Joseph considered the Church of England to be the perfect answer to Rome and Puritanism, as it sat quite comfortably between the two. Poor Joseph was to find himself reproving of his old friend's intervention – however well meaning its intent. The truth of the matter is that Joseph went to considerable lengths to urge all Protestant controversialists to unite with him against Rome, rather than stand divided. I think we can draw the conclusion from this statement that Joseph could occasionally appear to be looking both ways – but how else could he expect to be perceived for all his endeavours to find the ideal *via media* in this difficult terrain? To say the least it made for an awkward life.

An award of Arms

By 1631 Bishop Hall considered himself worthy enough to apply for his own exclusive coat of arms. A portrait had been engraved of him ca. 1627 by J. Sampson and this illustration had been used in a book published by Philemon Stephens and Christopher Meredith in 1628. This very fine engraving must surely have been specially produced to mark Joseph's appointment as Bishop of Exeter in 1627 and it clearly contains the arms of the see of Exeter, (a vertical sword in front of two crossed keys for St Peter – the patron saint of Exeter Cathedral) in the top left corner. However, the shield on the opposing side was shown blank. Convention said that this position was reserved for the personal arms of the individual depicted. As

yet Joseph did not have that distinction. This is a very fine portrait of Joseph but apart from his fine spaded beard, that blank shield stands out a mile! No wonder he applied for his own personal arms.

His application was approved and a coat of arms was drawn up by *'Clarenceux, King of Arms, in the name of Charles by Grace of God King of England, Scotland, France and Ireland. A shield to the Rt. Revd. Joseph Hall and to the descendents of his body'.*
[Image © Emmanuel College Cambridge]
The design consisted of three Talbot's heads erased (that is to say wavy neck bases - not straight cut) in silver on a black ground. The

Talbots, (a breed of hunting dog now extinct) were displayed with their crimson tongues extended. Above the shield appeared a helmet and coronet and a lion rampant. No one knows for sure but some historians hold a view that the Talbots were chosen by Joseph in affectionate memory of King James I whose favourite pursuit was hunting with hounds.

This next picture, (together with shield close up) shows Joseph seated in his study at Norwich. It is likely to have been one of if not *the* very last portrait made of him. It was used as the frontispiece in his book *'Select Thoughts; or, Choice Helps for a Pious Spirit'*, (1654). Joseph died only two years after this publication appeared. It clearly shows Joseph sitting at his writing desk holding a pen in his right hand as if he were writing – even though the book seems to be either already written in or printed. Joseph is looking quite pensively serene with his gaze appropriately a meditative one and not focussed on the viewer. Of real interest here is the depiction of his coat of arms in the top right of the frame. We see it here with his three Talbot dogs, (right) impaled with the three-mitred arms of the see of Norwich, (left). Of course, the precious Dort medal has its place of prominence pinned to his breast as usual. At the time of this book's publication Joseph had owned this much-loved medal for thirty-five years.

Also of interest in this picture is the appearance of part of Joseph's library of books – always considered then a mark of great status. One fascinating thought is that maybe most, if not all of the books displayed would have been the very items taken away from him in 1643 when his precious books and just about everything else he owned, were seized by order of sequestration. This sad situation with its happier outcomes is detailed in *Chapter Four*. The sharp-eyed reader will notice that none of the works appear to have bound spines. The straightforward reason for this is that publishers did not always bind all their public sale volumes. It was cheaper to purchase a book in final folded format with the sections sewn at the spines, but left unbound. The cost in the early 17th century of a 4to -sized book, (roughly A4) comprising a few hundred pages might well be 30/-, (£1.50) fully bound, and 12-15/-, (60-75 pence) without bound covers. Quite an attractive saving and many people would have adequately bound their own copies. It looks as though Joseph may well have gone for the unbound alternative on the evidence of what we can see in his bookcase. It goes without saying that he would certainly have had presentation copies fully bound if they were destined to be given to people of status. There is more information about the extent of Joseph's library collection in *Chapter Five* under the contents of his will.
(Illustrations above taken from a print in the author's collection).

Bishop Hall's grave pronouncement

Whilst at Exeter, Joseph Hall first expounded his strong view against church burials. He much preferred the use of churchyards for this and all the better if situated outside the town or city perimeter. His only exception would be . . . *"for princes and great persons . . . who have their private chapels for their repositories."* We shall see that he held to this view all his life, even to the point of having a special instruction left in his will regarding his own final resting place.

Joseph's main objection to bodies buried within churches was on the grounds of sanitation. He also believed it was not theologically proper either. He cited St. Swithin, buried without the cathedral walls at Winchester and recalled that this great saint " . . . *gave charge when he died that his body should not be laid within the church, but where the drops of rain might wet his grave and where passengers might walk over it – an example worthy of our imitation. There can no vault be so good to cover our graves as that of heaven.*" (See *Chapter Five*).

When he was called upon to consecrate a new burial ground in 1637, Joseph again pronounced that burial in open ground was preferable to interment within church buildings. The sheer numbers of souls being buried in the existing area in Exeter brought about the need for this additional cemetery. The date of the event was 24th August, which is St. Bartholomew's Day. In *Chapter Five* we shall see that a certain church in Norwich dedicated to this saint would yet prove to be his sanctuary during a time of painful exile. However, on this day in 1637 bishop Hall dedicated '*Bartholomew Yard*' in an area of Exeter then known as '*Little Britayne*'. A contemporary chronicler, Samuel Izacke, recalled:

> "*A new Church yard, on 24th August, St Bartholomew's Day, was solemnly consecrated by Bishop Hall, a piece of Ground formerly called Friern-hay lying within the Walls of the said City, and levelled and enclosed by the concurrent charge of both Church and City, by the cause and vigilance of the Mayor*".

The records tell us that Exeter Cathedral paid £150 for the land to be cleared and prepared, and the City authorities forwent £13 per year rent, as their part in the shared venture.

Controversies – rebuttals and conciliation

In 1640 Bishop Hall addressed the 'Long Parliament' with a direct defence of the liturgy and the Episcopal order of the House of Bishops. He very firmly asserted the Anglican standpoint whilst also holding out an olive branch to his opponents:

> '*Alas, my brethren, while we do fully agree in all these and all other doctrinal and practical points of religion, why will ye be so uncharitable, as, by these frivolous and causeless divisions, to rend the seamless coat of Christ? Is it a title, or a retinue, or a*

ceremony, a garment, or a colour, or an organ pipe, that can make us a different Church, while we preach and profess the same saving truth?"

Joseph Hall courted controversy by holding to principled and somewhat divergent views from the majority of bishops. It must nevertheless have struck him as a bit rich, when Laud, his old adversary, came to rely on his good will and debating skills when the power of the House of Lords was challenged, fuelled, in the main, by malicious pamphlets and sermons which commonly called for its demise. Laud was shrewd, for he realised that Joseph Hall could speak with convincing authority on this matter.

In many ways Joseph was the perfect conciliator. However, the task was great, for the tide against the power of bishops was rising steadily. It soon became apparent that the time for wise and gentle counsel had passed, for, on November 3rd 1640, Archbishop Laud was impeached for treason and for obstructing the King's access to his members of Parliament. Within days the powerful and hitherto untouchable Archbishop Laud was hauled off to the Tower to await his fate. He would not actually face trial until 1644. He was to receive the ultimate sanction when he faced the block in 1645.

The 'Smectymnuus' Controversy

Whilst Laud was immured the conciliatory Bishop Hall still valiantly strived to be heard as a lone voice as nationally heated debate almost engulfed him. In speaking up for Archbishop Laud's view Hall knew he was at risk of being the focal point of vindictive responses, and so it turned out. When he went into print with *'An Humble Remonstrance to the Court of Parliament, by a Dutiful Son of the Church'* the reaction from Laud's detractors was swift and vindictive. They went into print with a rebuttal to Hall in the first of a number of pamphlets which were written anonymously by a select group of five divines. This whole unsavoury episode was to become known as the *'Smectymnuus' Controversy*.

This weirdly absurd name was derived from the aggregation of the initials of the unspecified Puritan clergy, who commenced a very bitter public character assassination on bishop Hall. Already distressed by this nasty affair it must have further smarted because the cowardly individuals were not prepared to be identified. The whole public spat took place via a series of pamphlets, which at first were based upon countering Hall's defensive position regarding the validity of the Episcopate. However, the terseness of the vile and scurrilous later publications was pointedly aimed at destroying his personal standing over and above the original reasoning. Joseph was deeply hurt by this vindictiveness - so much so that he courageously withdrew from the unsavoury affair on the basis that he would not, could not, lower himself to the depths of his adversaries. Joseph was to go to his grave some fifteen years later never knowing for sure who these wicked individuals were. They may have cloaked themselves with secrecy at the time, but historians are now certain from other evidence that the anonymous *Smectymnuan* individuals were:

> **S**tephen **M**arshall
> **E**dmund **C**alamy
> **T**homas **Y**oung
> **M**atthew **N**ewcomen
> **W**illiam **S**purstow

NB To make the leading initials correctly spell out 'SMECTYMNUUS' it is necessary for the 'W' of William Spurstow to be written as it sounds - with two, (double) UUs. Deviously clever. Thomas Young was Scottish and a former tutor of John Milton, who we will see was definitely supporting the attacks on Joseph Hall via the *Smectymnuus-five* . The other four were English.

The published altercations between Hall and the *'Smectymnuus'* group went something like this:

> **Hall** – *'An Humble Remonstrance to the Court of Parliament, by a Dutiful Son of the Church '*(1641*)*.
> **'Smectymnuus'** - *'An answer to a booke entitled, 'An Humble Remonstrance', In Which, the Origin of Liturgy and Episcopacy is Discussed'.* (March 1641)
> *(To which book John Milton is now known to have added the post scrip – anonymously, of course).*
> **Hall** – *'A Defence of the Humble Remonstrance, against the frivolous and false Expectations of Smectymnuus'.* (1641*)*.

Smectymnuus – *'A Vindication of the Answer to the Humble Remonstrance, from the Unjust Imputations of Fivolousnesse and Falsehood'*. (1641).

Not to be outdone, John Milton also weighed in to defend his friends within 'Smectymnuus' with two published tracts:

> *'Animadversions upon The Remonstrants Defence Against Smectymnuus'* (1641*)* and
> *'Apology for Smectymnuus'*. (April 1642).

(NB The use of the word *'Apology'* in the aforementioned titles refers to its alternative use as an expression of written or spoken *defence*).

Although Joseph's withdrawal from active participation in the nasty campaign against him had effectively taken the heat out of the situation, one of his sons, (believed to have been Robert Hall) came to his defence only to attract vile scorn himself from John Milton. Although the printers must have been glad of the business they must also have been relieved at the cessation of this episode, for they surely would have soon run out of type for those ever more extravagantly worded titles!

On the second Sunday of Lent 1641, Bishop Hall preached before King Charles I at Westminster. By all accounts it was a remarkable sermon with its text being, *'The Mischief of Faction, and the Remedy of it'*. Knowing that the opposing voices were rising in passion, this mild and tolerant man tried his best to plead for sanity and reasonableness. He lamented the frenzy of the extremists on both sides knowing full well that he would again get the full force of their ranting. In fact he proclaimed that he was happy to be censured by them, for he saw his rôle to be that of cement between blocks of masonry. Opposing stones could never stand as a unified whole without their need to be in direct contact with the mortar. A neat argument.

Bishop Hall returns to Exeter – for the last time

In the summer of 1641 Bishop Hall returned from Westminster to Exeter where he still enjoyed the love and respect of its people. He recalls that he was: *"Cheerfully welcomed with some hundreds"* of supporters. He was not to know that this was to be his very last visit to Exeter for, very soon after his return to Westminster for the Autumn session of Parliament, came the news of his appointment by King Charles I to the Bishopric of Norwich.

The impending Civil War was set to engulf Exeter between 1642 and 1645 when Parliamentary forces besieged this historic city, with Fairfax accepting the final surrender in 1646. Joseph Hall, with his leanings towards the churchmanship of King Charles I, was at least spared the turmoil in Exeter after its ultimate fall to the Parliamentarians. The King was a shrewd man. His action in translating Bishop Hall from Exeter to Norwich was a very well balanced judgement. The royal plan was to install bishop Joseph Hall, the renowned conciliator into a diocese that for the previous nine years had endured neglectful governance and conflict at the hands of either lax or overbearing bishops.

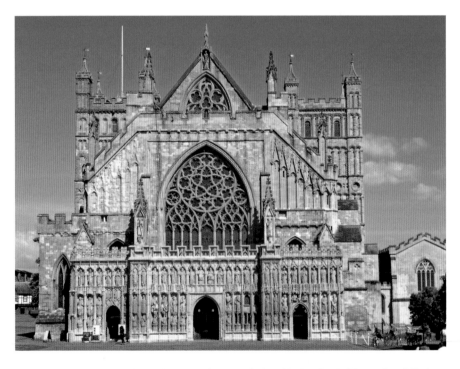

The very imposing Gothic west front of the Cathedral Church of Saint Peter, Exeter, Devon, where Joseph Hall was consecrated Bishop on 23rd of December 1627.

CHAPTER FOUR

(1632-1647) Turbulence - the Tower – the 'Delinquent' Bishop
Wreckers in Norwich Cathedral – 'Hard Measure'

We have to correctly understand the turmoil of the diocese that Joseph Hall was about to inherit to fully appreciate what he had to contend with on his translation to Norwich, where most of the problems in the diocese prior to 1641 were certainly created by his immediate predecessors. However, one person above the rest was responsible for a good deal of the tensions in the Church at large - the overbearing William Laud. It will be useful to digress here for a moment whilst we gauge his influence within the church, the state and the lives of worshipping individuals.

William Laud

William Laud had achieved quite a spectacular rise within the Church. He entered St. John's College, Oxford in 1589. His tutor there was John Buckeridge – an ardent hater of Puritanism. This fact cannot be disconnected from Laud's future behaviour towards such individuals. Buckeridge may well therefore have a great deal to answer for. Laud was elected a fellow in 1593. He was appointed Dean of Gloucester in November 1616. He had direct contact with royalty when he accompanied King James I on a Scottish Mission in 1617. Interestingly, Joseph Hall, then the Dean of Worcester, was also in the accompanying party.

Laud's first bishopric was that at St. David's in Wales in 1621. On 2nd February 1626 he gained prominence at the Coronation of King Charles I who had preferred him to attend over the head of the Bishop of London, (John Williams) who was out of favour with the King at the time. It is unlikely that Laud was embarrassed over this, which probably means that he didn't suspect that His Majesty apparently did not much like him either, but felt obliged to endure him for the sake of the ceremony. It must have therefore surprised many when he was appointed Bishop of Bath and Wells within weeks of the Coronation.

In 1627 Laud made it onto the Privy Council from where he could be in regular and intimate contact with the King and be involved with national decision-making as well as organising spying against Joseph Hall in the Exeter Diocese. Within a year he was translated to Bishop of London, (1628) and, only five years later on 19th September 1633 he was appointed Archbishop of Canterbury. As Primate of the Church of England he now had unlimited powers – and would come to use them.

Without delay Archbishop Laud issued instructions to all clergy regarding reverence, decency and the good ordering of divine services. Some, on the face of it, looked to be rather petty. For instance, the font water was to be clean and there were to be no more instances of *'wicker bottles and tavern pots'* being seen at the communion table. The parish clerk's reading abilities were to be tested in order to judge his capability of clearly leading the congregational responses. The parish perambulation, (beating the bounds) was only to take place during the Rogation Days, (Easter to Ascension) in the church calendar.

We now need to resume our survey of governance in the Norwich Diocese during the nine years before Joseph Hall was appointed as its bishop.

Bishop Corbett translates to Norwich in 1632

Much of the antagonism within the Norwich Diocese after 1632 was due to the corrosive exploits and actions of two recent bishops – Richard Montague, and before him the infamous Matthew Wren. However, preceding them the diocese had been placed in the hands of the rather ineffectual Richard Corbett, who became Bishop of Norwich in 1632. Corbett had been Bishop of Oxford for three years before translation to Norwich. He was by all accounts a very un-clerical man, indeed we might these days consider him a bit of a cove. He was prone to excessive drinking, merriment and practical joking! His temperament and demeanour were therefore not in keeping with that expected of a bishop. Neither was he a good example of pious living either. His somewhat limp image was not strengthened in the view of his detractors by the fact that he was by all accounts a rather good poet. Laud already had a distinct disliking of Corbett's casual Episcopal management and had duly noted his appointment to Norwich in 1632. As Bishop of London at the time he did not have the power to act against him, but all that would change the very next year with his appointment as Archbishop of Canterbury. Bishop

Corbett must have fearfully expected prying within his diocese to be inevitable.

By 1635 Laud was in an all-powerful position within Church and government and soon started to impose his will regarding matters of ceremony and practice. The nation at large considered his doctrines to be rather 'Popish'. For instance, Laud ruled that in future the pulpit was not to be the dominant feature of a church for he ordered that the communion table would instead henceforth be the principal focus. Puritan lecturers were to be suppressed. The Irish and Scottish Churches were forced to agree and sign their allegiance to a document that clearly stated that their future governance would be by Archbishops, Bishops, Deans and Archdeacons. Not a popular move.

Laud's inquisitor Brent reaches Norfolk in 1635

Two years prior to this in 1633 Archbishop Laud had appointed *Sir Nathaniel Brent* to spearhead his investigations into suspect bishops. It was quite a task and Brent did not reach Norfolk until the Spring of 1635. Bishop Corbett must have been rather concerned about the arrival of Laud's man in his diocese. One imagines that much bad news must have been heard about these inquisitions from across the country, and whispers must have preceded Brent wherever he went, for his commission aroused anxieties in many a diocese – and none more so than here in Norwich.

Bishop Corbett must at least have hoped that the commencement of Brent's investigations would be uneventful. Sadly, this was not to be the case. Brent was very displeased with the offhand way he was greeted in Norwich. He rebuked the council and reported to Archbishop Laud that: " . . . the mayor and his brethren came not to visit me at my coming in. Afterwards I convented, [summonsed] them for walking indecently in the Cathedral church every Sunday in the prayer-time before the sermon, and I admonished them to forbear for the future. . . . After this they visited me often . . . protesting they will be always ready to desire your Graces' good opinion of them". At the cathedral Brent found that: " . . . The hangings, [tapestries] of the choir are naught, the pavement not good, the spire of the steeple is quite down, the copes are fair but want mending. The churchyard is very ill-kept".

Brent's description of the spire is very confusing, if not a little misleading. The records would suggest that although a top portion of the spire was indeed missing, it was no more than six feet at the very most. Blomefield has it that the spire was definitely damaged by a storm in 1629, and that a Chapter meeting in 1633 had agreed to its repair. What we must surmise from Brent's observation therefore is that by the time of his visit in 1635, (six years after the damage) the agreed repair work had obviously still not been put in hand. Brent also went on to say that: *". . . many ministers appeared without priests' cloaks, some of them are suspected for non-conformity, but they carry themselves so warily that nothing can be proved against them"*.

During 1635 Archbishop Laud made a pronouncement about the Dutch and French Churches in the Kingdom. They were henceforth ordered to conform to the Church of England or be doubly taxed for resisting. The detail of this demand must have bewildered all those to whom it concerned. All 'native' members of their congregations born in England, being therefore the King's subjects, must hereafter leave their Dutch or French congregations and worship in their respective Church of England parish churches. Furthermore, those of Dutch or other foreign birth, would be free to stay in their worship centres, but they must in future use the English liturgy, translated into their own language if necessary. On the face of it this all looks to be a bit too much to ask and to organise. How, for instance, would such a scheme be adequately monitored to ensure the directive had been conformed with? Religious worship was beginning to get a bit complicated in Norwich, as elsewhere. Things could only get worse.

Of course, the irrepressible Brent was only too pleased to inform the foreign non-conformist gatherings in Norwich of Archbishop Laud's reproof. He duly reported to His Grace that: *". . . the Dutch and Walloon congregations are admonished according to your Grace's directions . . ."* Whilst all this upheaval was being concentrated in his diocese the strain and stress on Bishop Corbett must have been severe. It cannot therefore be a coincidence that, within three months of Brent's arrival in Norwich, Bishop Richard Corbett was dead. His demise must have been greeted by Laud as a golden opportunity to place one of his ardent supporters and admirers into the now vacant Norwich bishopric. To be utterly fair to Brent it must be recorded that he did not personally and definitively criticise Corbett in his report to Laud. This could not have been to Laud's liking for he had no hesitation whatever in later relating to His Majesty that the Norwich diocese under Bishop Corbett "... *was in total disorder".*

Bishop Matthew Wren 'the unclean bird' – lands in Norwich

Because the very easy-going Corbett had attracted Laud's prying attention to the Norwich Diocese we cannot dismiss the likelihood that he ultimately contributed to the disorder that was to follow him. Life for the worshippers in the Norwich Diocese was set to become calamitous. At the death of Bishop Corbett, Matthew Wren, *(pictured left)* was currently Bishop of Hereford. He was very much a staunch Laudian and therefore considered the perfect choice to get to grips with the 'errant' Norwich diocese. Wren, who took office without much delay in 1635, was described by Clarendon as *"a man of a severe, sowr nature, but very learned."* Wren was totally inflexible in his drive to force his, (and Archbishop Laud's) measures upon all the flock in his new diocese. During Corbett's Episcopacy local people had no doubt quietly 'just got on with things.' A new regime of serious over-management was set to seriously jolt them.

Wren was callously critical of non-beneficed preachers who he regarded as *"vagrant priests and trencher-chaplains".* This latter term was a derisive comment and widely applied to priests who were to be found working as tutors in large country manors and considered to be no better than 'hangers-on'. In fact, Joseph Hall himself had also taken a satirical swipe at trencher-chaplains in his poem *'The Domestic Tudor's Position.*

A gentle squire would gladly entertain
Into his house some trencher-chapelain,
Some willing man that might instruct his sons,
And that would stand to good conditions.
First, that he lie upon the truckle-bed
Whiles his young master lieth o'er his head.
Second that he do on no default
Ever to presume to sit above the salt.
Third that he never change his trencher twice.
Fourth that he use all common courtesies;

Sit bare at meals and one half rise and wait.
Last, that he never his young master beat,
But he must ask his mother to define,
How many jerks she would his breech should line.
All these observed he could contented be,
To give five marks and winter livery.

In this pithy poem Joseph is clearly saying that the trencher-chaplain is a
bit of a toady who, so long as he observes minimal rules of the household,
can expect a comfortable living under the master's roof, plus 5 marks
(about three pounds) a year and a new set of clothes at winter-time. The
reference to truckle-bed infers that the chaplain will sleep on a low bed,
which was normally stored under the main bed. He had to be mindful of his
'place' by sitting some distance from the expensive salt container when at
table, and was to use only one plate for all courses. Further, he was
expected to wait at table if asked, and always to keep his head uncovered.
Finally, the writer cannot resist the satirical comment that the 'disciplining'
of the student by his tutor is likely to be a complete sham, for he is
expected to ask the mother first how much padding should be put down the
lad's breeches - before any corrective beating is administered! I think
Joseph makes his points well – a trencher-chaplain was a yes-man; always
too lenient to his charge; never engaged in a real day's work – but
nevertheless faring undeservedly well.

Some of Wren's enforced measures were regarded as Popish and
superstitious by a large number of his flock. His abrasive attitude towards
Puritans caused several disturbances in East Anglia. Eventually, the
pressure on Puritans was so severe that they felt obliged to seek refuge by
emigrating to Holland and to New England. This is why a large number of
locations in Connecticut and Massachusetts still bear East Anglian place-
name connections. Francis Lawes, a weaver from Hingham in Norfolk,
sailed for New England with his young servant-lad Samuel Lincoln, who
was to become a forefather of the great Abraham Lincoln. Not content with
his attacks on Puritans, Wren also turned his venom upon the Dutch and
Walloon congregations, in a continuation of the hostile attitude already
shown to them by Laud and his Inquisitor-General, Brent, a year or so
before. The sad result was that many of the immigrant 'Strangers' felt
obliged to return to those countries on the continent from which they had
escaped a century before owing to persecution. Although Wren's stay in

Norwich was to be somewhat brief, those three years must have seemed much longer to those who suffered his presence in the county.

In 1636 Bishop Wren issued his *'Orders, directions and remembrances'* which amounted to twenty-eight articles, all of which fully supported the national stance taken by Archbishop Laud regarding church governance and observance of ritual. New rules and orders were continually being enforced on worshippers within the Norwich Diocese. The more they heard the name of Bishop Wren, the greater their dislike of him grew. One particularly unpopular decree concerned the construction and novel introduction of the altar-rail.

Wren's imposition of this barrier 'twixt altar and worshippers, was apparently a remedy he had contrived in answer to the problem of large numbers of stray dogs wandering into churches and defiling the altar table legs! One wonders why an order to ensure that all doors were correctly closed hadn't been seen as a more effective means of solving the problem. Did Wren consider this canine vexation to be the perfect excuse for him to issue yet another overburdening ordinance? Worshippers in the Norwich Diocese were getting seriously fed up by now.

In only a short time Wren was to become, after Laud himself, the most hated of all the bishops. By way of mocking caricature Wren was anonymously referred to as *"the least of all those Birds, but one of the most unclean ones "* However, in 1638 Wren's harsh and unyielding reign in the Norwich Diocese was to end with his translation to the wealthier see of Ely, which, although not geographically far from Norwich, was removed sufficiently enough for the Norwich Diocese to rejoice that they were at last well rid of him. However, the newly emerging and worrying thought in the region must have been, who would succeed him? Could things get any worse?

Bishop Montague leaves Chichester for Norwich

The question of Wren's successor was settled when Richard Montague, (a man in his sixties) arrived in the Norwich Diocese shortly after Wren's departure in 1638. As soon as the identity of the new bishop was announced there must have been some serious foreboding, for Montague, a noted writer, scholar and theologian, was also known to be another from the same mould as the hated Wren.

The Norfolk population must have wondered if the King had misread or ignored their recent plight under Wren, for surely imposing Montague on them would be more of the same. After all, it had been said of Montague that he had *"a very sharp nib to his pen, and much gall in his inke against such as opposed him."* Montague had a record of chastising Puritans and Papists. He was a formidable pamphleteer and one of the chief controversialists of his age. His declared philosophy was to hold the middle ground between Puritan and Papist views and none would persuade him from this rationale.

Within a year of his arrival in Norwich he was faced with Norfolk stubbornness. His new flock were refusing to receive the holy sacrament at the dreaded altar-rails, which his despised predecessor had imposed. Perplexed, Montague sought Archbishop Laud's view on the matter. Laud conferred with Wren at Ely with the result that all clergy were instructed to conform to new rules regarding the distribution of the Holy Sacrament. Those wishing to receive Holy Communion were ordered to approach the altar and stand, as a body, in the chancel area: *". . . and as in course of civility and good order, it is seemly the best in the parish to come up first . . . the first rank to stand, sit or kneel, near or close unto the rails, which being the most eminent place, the best in the parish may fitly be disposed there".* The priest's function in this new order was to then pass along the rows of people and so administer the sacred elements with the 'worthiest' receiving first. No wonder there was hostility in conforming to this rule. Whatever happened to the belief that the first shall be last and the last shall be first, and that in the eyes of God all men 'stand' as equals?

However, as things were to turn out, those fatigued by the previous three years of constant strife under Wren were to have a quick relief from the new bishop, for Montague's health was set to deteriorate rapidly and he died in April 1641 from what was described as *'quartan ague'* – not dissimilar to a form of malaria. Whilst ailing it wouldn't have raised his spirits any had he known that exasperated opponents at St. Peter Mancroft Church in Norwich had petitioned Parliament against his authoritarian manner in inhibiting their vicar, John Carter, from preaching on Tuesdays in their church. The resulting Bill, which would have deprived Montague of his bishopric, and made him ineligible for ecclesiastical promotion, was set to be totally frustrated by Montague's ill-health which rendered him too weak to travel to London to face the charge. Within weeks Montague had died causing an anonymous chronicler to observe that he *"went a more compendious way to answer all in the High Court of Heaven"*.

Bishop Wren has his wings clipped

Elsewhere, Puritan MPs from East Anglia thought it an opportune moment to bring bishop Matthew Wren of Ely to account and impeach him if appropriate. Worshippers in the Norwich Diocese sensed that they were at last going to get a degree of retribution over a detested bishop. There was a fear that the *'unclean bird'* might take flight from impending justice so Parliament, wishing to frustrate such an attempt had Wren bound over under the sum of £10,000. The twenty-five articles of impeachment that Wren faced included:

> *The raising of altars upon steps at the east end of the chancel.*
> *The erection of the hated altar-rails.*
> *The removal of pews and other seats from the chancel area.*
> *The wearing of surplices.*
> *The use of bold, exaggerated bowing and 'superstitious gestures'.*

Also under review were the cases of former ministers who Wren had sacked or effectively silenced during his Episcopacy. Former emigrants to Holland and New England, (some of whom had returned to England when Wren left Norwich) were also called to give evidence against him. Not overlooked either was Wren's tampering with the official seal of the Norwich Diocese so as to include a 'Popish' image of Christ upon the Cross next to the emblem of the see.

After lengthy deliberation Wren was found guilty and sent to the Tower in December 1641. Such was the tide of feeling against him that he was forbidden to offer any defence. Although the sentence was lifted in Spring 1642 with Wren being allowed back to Ely for the summer months, he was re-arrested later that year and this time he would not set foot outside the Tower of London again for the next eighteen years. During this long Commonwealth incarceration he was never brought to trial. It is not fair to say he was forgotten about either, for there is evidence that Wren was offered terms for his earlier release, but, owing to his stubborn nature he refused to accept the details of the conditions. At the Restoration in 1660 he was released and allowed to resume his Episcopacy at Ely where he died in 1667, at the age of eighty-two.

After two detested bishops in the space of just five years the good folk of the Norwich Diocese had to hold their breath and wonder whom the King was going to dump on them next. King Charles I may well have feigned ignorance of the real situation in the Norwich Diocese at the time he appointed bishop Montague, but this stance would not possibly wash in Norwich for a second time, for the King must have been aware of the anti-Montague Bill frustrated in Parliament. King Charles I duly announced that the next bishop of Norwich would be the perfect choice to bring overdue reconciliation and moderacy of governance to the region. However, things did not immediately bode well for his chosen man!

New bishop detained in Tower debacle

The seven-month interregnum in the Norwich diocese was ended in November 1641 when Joseph Hall, (currently bishop of Exeter) agreed to his translation to Norwich. Confusingly, Joseph actually records the date in his note-book as being 16th December. Never mind, it's a mere detail of no significance when compared to the event shortly to bear down on him, for, prior to actually coming to Norfolk, he was caught up in a most worrying circumstance in London, which only served to illustrate just how bad the relationship had currently become between the bishops and the populace at large. 1641 saw a massive public swing away from the Commons and the Episcopacy in general. Even Joseph Hall, the supreme middle-way moderate, became embroiled in a national incident that was ultimately to lead to the withdrawal of his liberty.

He and several other prelates were very roughly jostled and jeered by a crowd of discontents who tried to restrain them from entering the House of Lords. The cry went up *"No bishops, no bishops!"* and the ensuing melee proved too much for Bishop Joseph Hall and his brethren to cope with, so they retired from the scene rather shaken, and not a little annoyed. Writing later about this incident Joseph said:

" . . .it was not for us to venture anymore to the House without some better assurance [security]".

The Archbishop of York, Dr John Williams, (very much an opponent of Laud) convened a meeting of the eleven frustrated bishops, and this body then petitioned the King for their guaranteed security in future when attending the House. Eleven bishops, plus the archbishop himself, signed the document. But this was not all, for they stipulated that any legislation passed whilst they felt obliged to stay away from Parliament owing to poor security, should be declared null and void. This was a very bad move and sadly proved that the bishops had totally misconceived the public mood. There was no way that special treatment and molly-codling of bishops was going to be tolerated. The King refused the petition and all twelve signatories were held in contempt of the House and impeached. Predictably, Archbishop Laud sought the highest sanction possible against them and pressed the charge of treason. They were summarily found guilty and had their land and incomes immediately forfeited to the Crown and were taken to the Tower of London to await their fate.

To pass their time constructively whilst thus confined, these holy men engaged in writing sermons, which they regularly preached to each other quite apart from every Lord's Day. Archbishop Laud and Bishop Wren from Ely were also immured here at this time and were possibly part of a captive audience on these occasions. Bishop Hall later recounted that they preached " . . . *to a large Auditory of Cittizens"*. Surely those incarcerated and obliged to endure endless sermonising from nearly a dozen prelates, may have considered this 'treat' to be part of their punishment regime!

Bishop Hall covers this harrowing episode of imprisonment in one of his autobiographies, and it is well to leave him to explain the prevailing circumstances:

> *"We poor souls, who little thought that we had done any thing that might deserve a chiding, are now called to our knees at the bar and charged severally with high treason; being not a little astonished at the suddenness of this crimination, compared with the perfect innocence of our own intentions, which were only to bring us to our due places in parliament with safety and speed, without the least purpose of any mans offence. But, now, traitors we are in all*

the haste, and must be dealt with accordingly: for, on December 30th [1641] in all extremity of frost, at eight o'clock in the dark evening, we are voted to the Tower: only two of our number have the favour of the black rod, by reason of their age: which though desired by a noble lord on my behalf, would not be yielded".

After several weeks in the Tower the imprisoned prelates were released by virtue of the fact that their five lawyers, (very decently appointed by the Lords) were quick to point out to the Upper House petitioners that the charge of treason was not entirely appropriate to the case against them. The bishops were very likely to win on appeal. The Lords, obviously aware that this might well be so, prevaricated endlessly so that the bishops' incarceration stretched from days into several weeks. The uncertainty of their safety and welfare must have weighed heavily on their minds, not to mention those of their respective families too. After considerable delay, the Lords took the decision to release them from the Tower, and found them London lodgings. The bishops were of course delighted and somewhat bemused by this sudden change in circumstance.

After the staleness of the air he had endured for weeks in the Tower, Bishop Hall decided that a good walk in St. James's Park would be rather appealing. By remarkable misfortune, whilst in the park, he was spotted by a member of the Commons. It had been this assembly that had originally forced their will onto the Lords, to have the bishops arrested. Unfortunately, the Commons had not been made aware of the decision to release the bishops; so immediate action ensued from an angered House of Commons to have the bishops apprehended. So, on that very night, all the released bishops were rounded up, re-arrested and taken back to the Tower. It is not difficult to imagine their distress at this dramatic reversal in their fortunes.

Meanwhile, in Joseph Hall's new diocese of Norwich, feelings within the population were running high. It would seem that the failure of Parliament to abolish bishops had had a surprising effect in Norwich where, instead of a languid acceptance of this national reversal of their wishes on the matter, the mood was sharpened in spite of it. During Lent 1642 the Dean and Chapter got wind of a potential uprising by apprentices, who it was believed were intent on attacking the cathedral to show their great dissatisfaction of the authorities there. Precautions were taken to keep a close watch on the city and the cathedral's security.

For all the whiff of rebellion, nothing actually happened, but it was nevertheless a clear sign of the twitchiness at the cathedral, and a true reflection of the hair-trigger atmosphere permeating amongst the citizens just beyond the confines of the walled Close. Remember, this anti-bishop phobia was a direct result of the five years the local population had endured at the hands of abrasive individuals who had recently occupied the bishops' palace. It should also be borne in mind that although their new bishop had been appointed in November of the preceding year, they had yet to set their eyes on him owing to his detention in the Tower of London some four months earlier on 31st December 1641.

Freedom, and so to Norwich - at last

On Whit Sunday in 1642 Joseph Hall and his fellow immured colleagues were at last informed that the original charge of treason had been reduced to a lesser one, and that a bail fee of £5000 per head would bring their release. So they were all finally free and Joseph was reunited with Elizabeth. This time, forgoing any thoughts of having a walk in the park, Joseph, Elizabeth and family made haste to leave London for Norwich. Surely life must be more tranquil in Norfolk?

[Norwich Cathedral from the south-west Cloister]

The Halls were not newcomers to East Anglia of course; Elizabeth was a Suffolk girl and Joseph had spent all those years in Hawstead where he met and married her. Sometime shortly after his release in London the Halls were in residence in the bishop's palace in Norwich. Joseph was in due course installed as Bishop of Norwich, succeeding Bishop Richard Montague. For about a year his suspended income was restored. We are led to believe that the cathedral congregation quickly warmed to him and listened to Joseph's sermons with great attention, discovering for themselves that he was a quite splendid preacher. 1641 and early1642 had been particularly traumatic years for the Halls - and things were not about to get any better with the harrowing death of their youngest son Edward on Christmas Eve 1642 - only a few months after their arrival in Norwich. Joseph and Elizabeth were understandably devastated. It is not difficult to feel their pain when reading a translation, (*see below*) of the deeply moving memorial plaque placed in Edward's honour on the north wall of the cathedral Presbytery, adjacent to the high altar. Somewhat miraculously it is still *in situ*, somehow surviving the 1643 desecration of the cathedral, during which many brass memorial inscription plates were quite probably removed and destroyed.

The Edward Hall memorial brass 'mystery'

Only two cathedral brasses pre-dating 1643 have survived beyond this awful episode. One of this miserable total is the one dedicated to Edward Hall. Its survival to this day is considered by some to be rather inexplicable. Why did it escape the attentions of those set upon ripping out other brasses in 1643? Did it not stand out a mile with its memorial reference to a recently deceased member of the Hall family – whose head had just been nationally identified and denounced by Parliament in derogatory terms? Will the prevailing circumstances of that awful year in the cathedral's history therefore stand fresh enquiry, and can this yield the reason for the plaque's existence in the cathedral Presbytery today? I think so.

A view that is sometimes offered is that Bishop Hall was forced to humble himself before the wreckers to plead that they should not remove his dear son's memorial brass, Surely it is distinctly unlikely that Joseph Hall would receive a sympathetic hearing from those intent on defacing the cathedral memorials? Remember, on the 23rd March that very year, Parliament had named him to be a *'delinquent'* and in consequence had placed a sequestration order upon him only four days later, as detailed below. This would have been fresh in the minds of those with whom he would have had to plead. Owing to the memorial's great significance to Joseph and his wife I am mystified that he left no comment about his undoubted fears and anxieties about this situation in any of his memoirs that I have studied. If he had indeed pleaded successfully for the plaque's survival, then surely he would have said so at some point. It would have been a significant triumph for him - and he would not have passed over it without mention in his many retrospective writings – believe me!

Be that as it may. There is however one theory I would advance which would seem to neatly unravel this mystery and finally settle the matter, dare I say, once and for all? To be convinced of this reasoning however it is essential we take a very detailed look at precisely what the despoilers and looters were actually allowed to damage within the terms of the Parliamentary Ordinance. The following were on the banned list:

Altar rails, (imposed 1636 by Bishop Wren);
Crucifixes and crosses;
Depictions of The Holy Trinity, the Virgin Mary or any Saint.

Reference to the Holy Trinity is particularly apt considering the dedication of Norwich Cathedral. We know for instance that brasses were removed from the Spencer Tomb in the Nave south aisle *(See illustration on page 74)* and that four of those brasses probably showed representations of Saints' Matthew, Mark, Luke and John at each corner position. The Wi(y)ndham tomb, (then situated in the Jesus Chapel – now to be found at the west end of the Nave north aisle) is also likely to have contained identical features at each corner of its huge slab top. Such brass depictions fell squarely within the checklist criteria of the wreckers and were therefore removed. I am minded to believe that the rule was interpreted strictly on the basis that the least degree of offensive iconic features encountered would render that tomb or memorial liable to automatic removal of *all* its brasses in the complete set thereon. Otherwise we would surely still have some odd *'acceptable'* brasses scattered around here and there on various stone slabs in the cathedral.

From this information it looks most likely that Edward Hall's small memorial brass fell outside the wreckers' terms of reference. It did not depict any iconography, and furthermore it was not attached to a tomb or grave slab. I believe this rather mundane explanation for the survival of this brass memorial is almost certainly the correct one. The only other possible reason for its survival is this. Owing to the young man's death being so late in the year, (Christmas Eve 1642) the brass may not have even been created and put in place until *after* the wreckers' visit on 12th May 1643. Knowing what a very sad year this memorial plate represents makes for it being a very moving and somewhat pitiful object to view. The inscription, in Latin and Greek, reads as follows:

Memoriæ S
Cultissimi inganii Speicq(ue) eximiæ
Νεογεφονη
Edouardo Hallo
Josephi filio natu minimo
Atum professori
Theologiæ Candidato
Pio, et Supra ætatem doctor
Posuere maesti PP
Tantum Eret
Vale lector, et æternitatem Cogita
Obiit in Vigiliis Nati
Salvatoris
Anno 1642
Ætatis vero, Suae
23°

[Sacred to the memory of Edward Hall, of the most cultivated intellect and of outstanding promise. Old before his time. Youngest son of Joseph Professor of Arts, Candidate in Theology, Pious and learned before his age. Take heed reader to mind eternity. He died on Christmas Eve 1642 in his 23rd year.
His sad parents placed this tablet]
Legend and translation by the late John Macdonald.
[Image above with permission. © Paul Hurst Photography]

Parliament declares Bishop Hall a 'Delinquent'

In 1643 Bishop Hall was variously named as either one of *'the delinquents'* or *'malignants'* who refused to denounce the Pope. He also strenuously defended the rights of King Charles I and the Constitution of the Realm plus the Holy Order of Bishops and the Church of England in general. He was to be utterly and mercilessly humiliated for having and holding onto his strong Christian and moral principles. On 1st April, (1643) Parliament issued an ordinance of sequestration against Joseph Hall which effectively stripped him of all income, including his rights to rent income from property he held in Norfolk, Suffolk and Essex. Every county was required to raise a committee and these bodies were invested with unrestricted powers of enquiry into the affairs of any individual. These committees were also empowered to sequestrate, (seize) personal goods as they saw fit. The enforcing sequestrators, appointed locally in Norfolk, have commonly been recorded with variable surname spellings – chiefly by Joseph Hall. I have given both versions initially then adopted the more modern alternative elsewhere.

Palace raided but true friends step forward

The individuals concerned were Mr Thomas Sotherton, Mr John [Tolye] Tooley (an Alderman, who had been Mayor of Norwich in 1638) Mr John [Rayley] Rawley (Sheriff) and Mr John Greenwood (Sheriff). Together with others in attendance they visited the Bishop's Palace. Before his own eyes the bishop witnessed the sequestrators going through every room, putting arbitrary values on all items in sight. Furniture, books, wooden dinner plates, window hangings, vestments, portraits of his children-nothing escaped. The only degree of leniency showed towards Joseph and Elizabeth was when the bishop implored of his obnoxious intruders that he and his wife be allowed to retain the clothes they were actually wearing! Grudgingly, Messrs Ward and Rawley agreed to this.

At the end of their sad incursion into the Hall's household, an inventory was drawn up so that all the goods listed thereon could be put up for public gaze and sale. Can anything be more humiliating than having to face up to the degrading prospect of witnessing one's items of personal and sentimental value being pored over at public auction? However, before this grossly distasteful action could be organised, a rather generous act of human kindness was to come the Halls way via a Mrs. Goodwin, (who was a resident in the Close) and who is believed to have been a sympathetic member of the cathedral congregation. Bishop Hall makes the following comment in one of his later books:

> " . . . *a religious and kind gentlewoman, whom yet we had never known or seen, being moved with compassion, very kindly offered to lay down to the sequestrators that whole sum which the goods were valued at, and was pleased to leave them in our hands for our use till we might be able to repurchase them; which she did*

*accordingly, and had the goods formerly delivered to her by Mr
Smith and Mr Greenwood".*

The virtuous lady concerned then forwarded the Hall's belongings back to
them and informed the bishop that he need only pay back to her whatever
he could afford, whenever he was able to. It is very likely that this kind
woman was a regular attendee at the cathedral and was no doubt amongst
those who had quite taken to Joseph since his arrival in Norwich.

In addition to the general household goods there were items arguably of
much more academic importance to Joseph – his books. It is not ridiculous
to think that he must have had copies of all his own books and pamphlets,
(probably at least thirty published titles in number by 1643) plus those of
other contemporaries, no doubt some foreign books too, plus, of course,
prayer books and bibles. It is quite likely that he had amassed a very
significant amount of manuscript notes too. For a learned man like Joseph,
being parted from his reference books and other documents would have
been a terrible sadness and frustration. Anyone with a love for - and need
of books, will testify to the truth of this.

Divine providence yet again intervened for Joseph, (and frustrated the
actions of the sequestrators) for when the books were offered up for sale,
nobody was interested in buying them. This immediate outcome didn't
directly help Joseph for his books were temporarily impounded and put
beyond his use. It is quite likely that the sequestrators had rather
mismanaged this would-be sale. Why did they think anyone was likely to
be interested in the books in the first place? Had they not considered that
the property of one they had declared to be a *'delinquent'* enemy of the
Church and state, might just be deemed a trifle risky to purchase and own?
After all, are we not very much intellectually identified with the contents of
our personal libraries?

Thank goodness for the intervention of yet another kindly soul. A Mr Cook
came forward and, having paid the sequestrators a sum they were content
with for Joseph's treasured books, promptly gave them back to a doubtless
delighted Joseph, who promised to pay back the benefactor as and when he
could from future financial allowances. There's no doubting the 'debt'
would have been eventually cleared. What a sad state of affairs the country
was in that it should seek to so humiliate and discredit such a worthy and
honourable man as Joseph Hall.

One simply has to admire the absolute courage and decency of Mrs. Goodwin and Mr Cook who both flew in the face of the pompous fanatics. There is no doubting the danger they put themselves in for showing such Christian kindness. Bishop Hall was particularly incredulous at Mrs. Goodwin's generosity as, by his own admission later, he had never seen or heard of her before in his life. If, as we suspect, Mrs. Goodwin was indeed a member of the cathedral congregation, it is quite likely that the bishop would not have been personally aware of her as it is almost inconceivable that she would have been on speaking terms with him. How many of us today are on common speaking terms with a bishop? Mrs. Goodwin was a good soul who knew when she was witnessing a decent man being unfairly vilified. Many honest folk must have also felt outraged by the serious damage to the much-loved cathedral. The world must have seemed like an evil place to Joseph, Elizabeth, their children and their supportive neighbours. These bold supportive gestures of defiance must surely have been very comforting, for without their stout aid the Hall's circumstances would have been dire indeed.

The act of sequestration had also taken away all of bishop Hall's income. How was he to support his wife and family? Joseph took the step of appealing against the lost income. He took his case to a sequestration committee when it was in session in Norwich. For a man almost stripped of all dignity, this was a desperate, almost despairing, act. Joseph cannot have had much faith that his appeal would have a satisfactory outcome. Against the odds the committee found in his favour and he won back an allowance of £400 per annum.

The officers who heard the case and showed this unexpected degree of leniency toward the bishop were Sir John Potts of Mannington, (representing the county) and Sir Thomas Wodehouse of Kimberley, (representing Thetford). In furtherance of their decision they submitted their findings to Edward, Earl of Manchester, who approved the matter forthwith by ordering that income from certain Episcopal lands should be set aside to yield the £400 yearly grant. A bishop at this time is likely to have received an annual income of £1200-£3000 depending on the appointment location.

When news of the apparent leniency showed to the bishop by the appeals committee in Norwich reached London it was held in contempt. Miles

Corbett, the rather odious MP for Great Yarmouth, whose high-handed and doctrinaire manner had seen him assume weighty powers on the Central Committee for Sequestration in London, ordered his colleagues to reverse the decision reached in Norwich, thus removing all of the £400 recently awarded to Bishop Hall whose later recollection of this setback recalls the news was delivered in writing by *'a Serjeant Wild'*. Clearly hopes of reasonableness dashed once more.

Bishop Hall invited to eat his books!

Sadly, news on this vexed matter was set to get even worse. The haughty power-crazed Miles Corbett was not content to leave matters there. He pronounced that such a despised and discredited individual like the bishop of Norwich was not fit to live in a palace. Corbett sent word that the Halls were to be informed their eviction from the palace was imminent. Only three weeks was granted to them in which to find other suitable accommodation. If they were still in the palace after that period of grace, Joseph and all his dependants would be summarily ejected onto the street. Joseph was forced to plead that they be allowed to rent the palace for a bit longer, but this was dismissed. The eviction order stood. When the poor man cringingly asked of them how was he to provide food for his family, the answer came back *" . . . go and eat your bookes'*.

Mrs. Hall was advised to plead to this same committee to see if they would award her an allowance for herself and her children. She was advised that, in such cases, only one fifth of her husband's allowance, (£400 per annum) could be paid to her on appeal. Her application was granted and she was awarded £80 per annum based on the above formula. She and her family were going to have to somehow subsist on roughly £7 per month. Typically, even this 'agreement' never came into force for, whilst prevaricating on the commencement of this pitiful amount it was discovered, (surely not surprisingly) that the Hall's finances were in such a mess that the adjudicators could not easily work out what the fifth part actually was. The Halls had ultimately to accept a figure that was less than the fifth part. It is conceivable that the final payment equated to no more than £6 per month. Even after this numbingly inadequate amount was settled, the actual payment of it was subjected to endless wrangling. Certainly a grim outcome and prospect for the Halls. Joseph later recalled:

"They were not ashamed, after they had taken away all my goods and personal estate, to come to me for assessments and monthly payments for that estate which they had taken; and took distresses from me upon my most just denial; and vehemently required me to find the wonted arms [alms?] of my predecessors, when they had left me nothing".

Bishop Hall resolves to do his duty

During all this bitter unpleasantness Joseph Hall still somehow maintained his office of bishop by resolutely continuing to ordain ministers and appoint others to the various clergy vacancies in his diocese, during ceremonies held in private. You couldn't blame him for this as he was still legally entitled to fees for such undertakings. Not surprisingly, this did not meet with general approval everywhere. As soon as his local detractors were made aware of what he had been secretly doing they took action against him. The enacting of the Universal Covenant on 2nd February 1644 saw hostile officers visit the bishop demanding the names of all the individuals he had ordained privily in this manner. Of course the bishop refused to acquiesce.

For his stubbornness he was informed he would have to appear before the Mayor to explain his actions. Bishop Hall absolutely refused to accede to this request. He sent word that he considered it quite preposterous and contemptuous for anyone to expect that a bishop would ever be answerable to a Mayor! He felt moved to write: *"I knew mine own place, and would take that way of answer which I saw fit: and so dismissed them . . ."* In fact, I have inspected a document at the Norfolk Record Office which is pertinent to the topic under review. It quite clearly states that Joseph Hall, Bishop of Norwich, Instituted John Alexander to the Rectory of Alderton, Suffolk, in 1648. This is such a late date that it does give credence to the possibility that bishop Hall was indeed by then conducting such ceremonies at his palace in Heigham. This document is actually signed 'Heigham' and is further commented on in *Chapter Five*.

During the spring of 1644 Bishop Hall laments on the sadly desolate condition of the cathedral: *" . . . now open on all sides [broken windows] to be filled with musketeers, waiting for the Mayor's return, drinking and tobacconing as freely as if it had turned alehouse."* This statement is open to varied interpretation depending on whether the account describes waiting for the Mayor, or, the *Major*- the original document being unclear. Most researchers are minded to take the word in question as being Mayor, for we know that the Mayor and the Corporation now attended the cathedral occasionally following its recent re-ordering of the furniture to their will. The layout of the presbytery had been altered so that the Aldermen sat at the east end and, in front of them, (where the high altar now stands) was the Mayor's seat. The Founder's Tomb, so recently desecrated and significantly damaged during the 1643 outrage, was now considered an inconvenient obstruction, and was almost completely dismantled.

Intrusive hostilities are relentless

One day, after the servants had been dismissed, a trooper from London called Wright arrived in the Close and demanded admittance to the palace. He stated he was under orders to search for unlicensed weapons. Two legally held items were found and Wright confiscated them. The stables were also searched. The bishop, who owned two horses, was told they were also to be seized. Being unable to travel to collect provisions for his household without a horse he pleaded for their retention. With great reluctance trooper Wright relented and allowed Joseph to keep the worst of the animals. And so the harassment against this fine and principled man, and his family went on.

Following this incident bishop Hall was visited in the Close by an unruly fanatical mob of local Puritans led by the Sheriff, Thomas Toftes, and Aldermen Messrs Linsey and Greenwood. Bishop Hall, who was in his palace at the time, was summoned to his private chapel and informed that his visitors were minded to search his property. Joseph later recalled that:

> "... *many zealous followers came into my chapel to look for superstitious pictures and relics of idolatry; and sent for me, to let me know they found those windows full of images, which were very offensive, and must be demolished. I told them they were the pictures of some ancient and worthy bishops, as St Ambrose, Austin etc. It was answered me that they were so many Popes".*

Joseph would appear to have argued successfully that should his unruly visitors have to damage his chapel's stained glass windows then surely they could spare the majority of the glass images by limiting their attention to the offending faces only. This we believe was the sad outcome. The status of the bishops' palace was to deteriorate steadily over the years following this incident. Quite apart from its inappropriate use for periods of time it was allowed to gradually fall into disrepair. During the Commonwealth period it was scavenged of its timbers, masonry and roof leads which were sold for scrap value. Included in the spoiling of this building was the destruction of its Great Hall built by Bishop John Salmon, (1299-1325). Bishop Hall's successor, Edward Reynolds, inherited such a derelict building at the Restoration that a largely new palace had to be erected for him ca. 1661.

In the Hall's moment of dire need, yet another good local soul stepped forward. A Mr Gostlin actually vacated his own home in The Close so that the evicted Halls could move into this property on a temporary basis. A *William* Gostlin was Mayor in Norwich 1643/44, and we know from the records that he was arrested and sent as a prisoner to Cambridge for questioning. The charge against him was for refusing to sanction what he thought were the excessive outrages of reformers in Norwich. To resist those who brandished such unbridled power was a defiant and courageous act. The Halls therefore duly moved from the palace to Mr Gostlin's house. It is difficult to know how long they remained there, but something like two years, (until 1645) is quite likely.

The damage to the windows of his palace chapel would have been bad enough for Joseph to endure but worse, much worse was to follow when the holy precincts of his beloved cathedral church received the ruthless attention of wrecking mobs of local Puritanical sympathisers. Joseph was almost getting used to desecration being perpetrated around him but the outrage unleashed on the cathedral fabric was heinous. He witnessed what actually happened and the famous Norwich dignitary Thomas Browne, (to later be knighted in 1671) also wrote of what he saw at that time.

Bishop Hall's 'Hard Measure'

Bishop Hall left a tragic twelve-page personal account of these sacrileges entitled *'Hard Measure'* which he dated 29th May 1647. In it he recounts:

*"There was not that care and moderation used in reforming the
Cathedral Church bordering upon my Palace. It is no other than
tragical to relate the carriage of that furious sacrilege, whereof
our eyes and ears were the sad witnesses, under the authority and
presence of Linsey, Toftes and Greenwood. Lord. What work was
here! What clattering of glasses! What beating down of walls!
What tearing up of monuments! What pulling down of seats! What
wresting out of irons and brass from the windows and graves!
What defacing of arms! What demolishing of curious stone-work,
that had not any representation in the world, but only the cost of
the founder, and skill of the mason. What tooting and piping upon
the destroyed organ-pipes! And what a hideous triumph on the
market-day before all the country; when, in a kind of sacrilegious
and profane procession, all the organ pipes, vestments, both copes
and surplices, together with the leaden cross which had been newly
sawn down from over the Green-yard pulpit, and the service-books
and singing-books that could be had, were carried to the fire in the
public market-place; a lewd wretch walking before the train, his
cope trailing in the dirt, with a service-book in his hand, imitating
in an imperious scorn the tune, and usurping the words of the
litany used formerly in the church. Near the public cross, all these
monuments of idolatry must be sacrificed to the fire; not without
much ostentation of a zealous joy, in discharging ordnance, to the
cost of some, who professed how much they had longed to see that
day. Neither was it any news, upon this guild-day, to have the
cathedral, now open on all sides, to be filled with musketeers,
waiting for the Ma(y)jor's return; drinking and tobacconing as
freely as if it had turned ale-house".*

It would be wise at this juncture to declare that confusion has long reigned
as to defining precisely the day on which the malevolent wreckers visited
the cathedral. The only solid clue is the date that Bishop Hall records in his
'Hard Measure' (finished 29th May 1647) where he identifies 12th May
1643. A persuasive corroboration towards accepting this date is provided
by the cathedral records which state that on 25th May 1643, four men were
paid for their toils in the removal of the hated organ, prior to its burning,
(amongst many other cathedral items) on a bonfire in the market place. We
therefore can presume that these individuals received their payment a few

days after the awful events of the 12th May. However, another factor also adds to the confusion of the precise date of the damage in the cathedral.

The Puritan-biased Parliament passed an Ordinance on 23rd September 1643 aimed at defacing or removing any image within a church or cathedral, which was considered idolatrous. Further, this draconian measure was set to expire on 1 November 1643. Therefore, with barely five weeks legality attached to any action, the systematic wrecking of monuments, fonts, windows and the like up and down the land was channelled into a very short period of time. Surely the brief life of the order was the main reason for the perpetration of so much wild, frenzied and hideous damage to Anglican buildings. Time was short - better get on with it. So does this leave us with the possibility that the damage was perpetrated in the cathedral in the later phase of 1643? It is very difficult to know. I think it safest to go with Joseph's date of 12th May 1643. He witnessed the grim event and is unlikely to have forgotten the date. Although *'Hard Measure'* was written at bishop Hall's palace at Heigham in 1647 I have not been able to verify that this very important 12-page booklet was published in his lifetime. I'm minded to believe its first publication was in 1660 when included in *'The Shaking of the Olive Tree'* - a posthumous publication of his works. *See pages 74 and 86.*

During the utterly appalling attacks on the cathedral's fabric, perhaps upwards of one-hundred individual brass plaques were torn from their fixings on tombs and memorials. Certainly this is the total arrived at by no less a figure than Dr Thomas Browne of Norwich who was an eye-witness to some of the outrage in the cathedral. Although vividly emotional, Bishop Hall's account sadly does not give any clue as to how many items were destroyed in the cathedral.

The figure that Dr Browne arrives at is disputed by modern historians who now believe some brasses were removed during the short reign of King Edward VI (1547-53). This could be a convincing argument if we accept one premise- that Dr Browne, (a parishioner of St. Peter Mancroft church in Norwich) was not that well acquainted with the cathedral's brasses *before* 1643. There is no doubting whatever that he witnessed *some* brasses being removed from tombs. I feel the issue is this - did he, in the undoubted high fever of watching this awful event, mistakenly count some already empty brass matrixes, (from the likely iconoclasm under King Edward VI) when arriving at his 1643 total? Frustratingly it is very doubtful we will ever know for certain.

What we have to realise is that the Puritans saw the glories of Norwich Cathedral as so much crude, offensive and iconoclastic paraphernalia. Far too Popish with its ornaments, vibrant coloured windows full of so-called saints, opulent tombs, monuments and carved images. They equally detested the high ceremony, the flowing robes and vestments, and also much loathed the tones of the organ and the chanting-men of the choir.

Even now, some three hundred and seventy years after those appallingly grim attacks on the cathedral's fabric, it is nigh on impossible to come to terms with how our forbears in this ancient city, albeit assisted by Cromwellian soldiers, could have brought themselves to the point of damaging and defacing precious artefacts within its treasured spaces. We know of course that not all the local populace supported this action, but, realistically, what opposition could they have effectively mounted against a large body of men, armed as they were with weapons, hammers and crow-bars, and so clearly set upon wilful acts of wanton aggression? Moderate minded Norwich citizens in the 1640s would undoubtedly have seen those zealous wreckers as the ASBO louts of their day!

We also have to remember that those intent upon defiling the sanctity of this great house of God, did so with the power of a Parliamentary Act to support them. It seems incredulous to us, but they were quite simply enforcing the law of the land as it stood at the time. The very fine cathedral, with its lofty piers and springing vaults, was to have its atmospheres of holiness shattered by the profane cheering of men about their infamous wrecking work. The grim and unrelenting echoes of hammer and crow-bar shattered the building's normal peaceful tranquillity, as the despoilers smashed and levered their way amongst the cathedral's defenceless tombs, graves, windows and memorials. The results of their dastardly toils are still shockingly chilling to observe today.

Bishop's calling not neglected

Even during such intolerable times Bishop Hall did not neglect his calling. He still tried his best to lead his people by public example. Adjacent to the Bishop's Palace was a Green Yard, which had been used for open-air preaching since at least the 1400s. Here Joseph and others would address their flock. It was a very popular place for Norwich citizens to go and hear sermons. Simple open-air wooden benches were provided for the ease of congregations and the use of such a seat could be obtained for the price of a silver penny. However, the more prestigious attendees were afforded a bit more in the way of comfort. If the Mayor, Aldermen or other local dignitaries were in attendance, they were housed within a wooden gallery, complete with a roof, which was built against the west-facing wall of the Bishops' Palace. A very similar lean-to construction was to be found erected against the outer north wall of the cathedral. This is where the Dean and his Prebendaries would sit, together with *". . . gentlemen, and the better sort".*

The focal point of the preaching area was the pulpit. This could be mounted via a series of stone steps, which took the preacher into the speaking chamber, which was mounted with a protective roof-cum-sounding board covered with lead to afford some weather protection. A large leaden cross surmounted the whole structure. It is believed that this pulpit in Norwich was in imitation of a similar construction outside Saint Paul's Cathedral, London. Sometime between September and November 1643 local Puritanical zealots turned their obnoxious attention on the Green Yard and uprooted the pulpit after first unceremoniously sawing off its leaden cross. In an act of profanity it was taken to an area outside the Black Friar's church, (modern day Saint Andrew's Hall in Norwich) where the pulpit was re-erected and subsequently used by Puritan preachers.

According to the records we know that Bishop Hall gave a public sermon on Whit Sunday 1644, from the Green Yard – by now without its pulpit. This incident probably took place immediately after the bishop's eviction from the palace. We are informed that the theme of this oration was *"Grieve not the Holy Spirit of God, by which ye are sealed to the day of redemption".* We also know he touched upon *"these heavy judgments, under which we have lain thus long"* during the address. This remark could easily be seen as a comment on his recent personal treatment. He went on to beseech his listeners towards prayer, penitence and fortitude, in the face of all the current tribulations. Perhaps this sermon's popularity was the reason for a repeat performance one month later in July 1644, when Joseph preached in the prestigious parish church of Saint Gregory, Norwich.

This picture shows the top slab of the tomb of Miles Spencer (d. 1569) showing the sad indentation remaining after the central figure-brass was sprung out of its rivets, very probably in May 1643, when wreckers ransacked 'offending' tombs, memorials and windows in Norwich Cathedral. *See page 61.*

Bifhop HALL'S

HARD MEASURE.

Othing could be more plain, then that upon the Gall of this Parliament, and before, there was a general Plot and Refolution of the Faction to alter the Government of the Church efpecially, the height and infolency of fome Church-governours, as was conceived, and the ungrounded impofition of fome Innovations upon the Churches both of *Scotland* and *England* gave a fit Hint to the Project : In the vacancy therefore before the Summons, and immediately after it, there was great working fecretly for the Defignation and Election as of Knights and Burgeffes, fo efpecially (beyond all former ufe) of the Clerks of Convocation ; when now the Clergy were ftirred up to conteft with, and oppofe their Diocefans, for the choice of fuch men as were moft inclined to the favour of an Alteration. The Parliament was no fooner fate, then many vehement Speeches were made againft eftablifhed Church-government, and enforcement of extirpation both root and branch. And becaufe it was not fit to fet upon all at once, the refolution was to begin with thofe Bifhops which had fub.

The Title page of Bishop Hall's *'Hard Measure'* as it appeared in *'The Shaking of the Olive Tree'*, posthumously published in 1660. *(See page 69).*

CHAPTER FIVE

Priestly 'retirement' to Heigham - final days and death - details of Bishop Hall's *will*

A new palace

Bishop Hall, Elizabeth, family and servants were ultimately forced from their cathedral palace in the Close where the evictors also saw fit to emphasise their evil vindictiveness by nailing up the front door to make any thought of immediate return impossible. To add insult to injury, as soon as the palace was vacated, the local Sequestration Committee moved in and made use of it. We also know that the building was sub-divided and let into tenements. In all, the building was put to much inappropriate use, including the opening of a tap-house in one room. One shudders to think what the bishop thought of all this.

The Halls eventually rented a substantial riverside house in the Hamlet of Heigham - on the north-western outskirts from central Norwich. This was to become their 'retirement' home for the next few years. Heigham was a busy little suburb and well known for its agriculture, farming, lime pits, corn milling and fisheries.

[Joseph's Palace at Heigham, Norwich, now known locally as 'The Dolphin' photographed by the Author in 2011]

At this point it might be as well to dispel the myth that has grown around which actual building in Heigham the Halls moved into, for I have seen there is some speculation about this. Having checked the records and other substantial pointers relating to this matter, I have to say that I believe dear old Joseph himself is perhaps   responsible for perpetrating any confusion there is owing to a comment he made once when writing to a colleague. The document carried a Latin phrase which, when translated, described that he was living in *"his little cottage"* in the parish of Heigham. This, almost certainly flippant remark, has led some historians to conclude Joseph was describing a much smaller building in the vicinity of Heigham. I am positive such a conclusion is wrong, for I am certain that the Halls went straightway to occupy the building that was later to become *The Dolphin Inn* (above) after they removed themselves from Mr Gostlin's house in Norwich Cathedral Close, sometime during the mid 1640s. A document in Norfolk Records Office, (NRO) states 1647 but gives no provenance for this information. As we shall discover below, this large house was worthy of a man of his importance and very fit for Joseph to consider as his palace-in-exile for the rest of his life.

I'm minded to say that Joseph's little joke has been distorted by academics that seem to have seriously latched onto what was undoubtedly a frivolously over-exaggerated, (even satirical?) remark by dear old Joseph. Let's not forget he was renowned for his wit. As we shall see in the following paragraphs, simply refuting the way this whimsical trifle has been interpreted is by no means all we have to go on to substantially support the idea that his palace was indeed the *'Dolphin'* building.

Richard Browne, (or, 'Brunne) who in 1595 was Sheriff of Norwich, commissioned the building in 1587. He was a Mercer by trade and his initials, *as depicted above*, can still be seen near the front door carved with the date 1587. Today local people know this famous landmark building as *'The Dolphin'*, but the first reference I could find to this name for the building is dated to 1802 when it is described as *The Dolphin Inn,* owing to there being an adornment on its structure at that time resembling this mammal. However, the authoritative Norwich pub researcher Derek McDonald has a reference to the building being a public house from 1715 –

but it was not then recorded as *The Dolphin*. There are other interesting records about this building, one of which would suggest that it was originally a large farmhouse *prior* to 1587. This would mean that Richard Browne probably developed one of the first ever barn conversions in Norfolk - something we previously thought was a very modern fashion!

Whatever the circumstances it was a rather spacious high status building. The physical structure we can admire today, (after its demise via German incendiary bombs in 1942) is a fairly tasteful 1960s rebuild. The local brewers, Steward and Patteson, (S&P) who owned the building at the time, paid for this refurbishment. A plaque on site, *(pictured left)* records this fact.

Other observations recorded in the 19th century by Walter Rye and others compellingly point to this building as having been Joseph Hall's palace, for there was a shield on the outer wall bearing the three-Mitre emblem of the see of the Norwich Diocese, and a carving depicting three Chalices and three Wafers. Symbols of the Holy Trinity - to which Norwich Cathedral is dedicated? Quite possibly. The previous existence of these emblems is conclusive to this having been the residence of Bishop Joseph Hall. The adjacent 'Old Palace Road' takes its name from the former bishop's house too.

In December 2010 the current users, (a Chiropractic clinic) granted me permission to view the main reception area in what I imagine was originally the ground floor lounge. Even allowing for its serious rebuilding and new décor in 1960 it still is an impressive space. All the original furnishings and lavish panelling were destroyed in the incendiary bomb attack during hostilities in 1942. However, a very grand and ancient fireplace with interesting carvings of shields and mysterious long-tailed dragons still survives. It's not hard to imagine old Joseph and Elizabeth warming themselves by its hearth all those centuries ago. Just inside the main door I was pleasantly surprised to discover an ornate carved recess, which I believe to be a holy water *stoup*, (possibly *piscina*) where visitors to this building in past centuries would have paused to dip their fingers before making the sign of the cross on their forehead, in an act of receiving a holy blessing via water which would have been previously specially

blessed. I remember this practice of 'spiritual cleansing' being observed by worshippers at just such a recessed niche at the rather 'high' church of St James Pockthorpe in Norwich, where I worshiped as a lad. The presence of this feature inside the old 'Dolphin' certainly fits well with its likely earlier existence in the palace of Joseph Hall. There is a local belief that this *stoup – (pictured left in 2010)* was brought here from the church of St. Bartholomew, Heigham, sometime after 1942. My judgement is that this cannot be so owing to the staggering bomb devastation within that church. An endorsement of this view is surely provided by published evidence that says it was in the old palace at Heigham in the late 19th Century. (Lewis – *A Life of Joseph Hall* page 407 pub. 1886).

Another source of proof for this building's status in the 17th century is contained in a manuscript held at Norfolk Records Office, (NRO). Whilst searching through a box of miscellaneous items I found an original Certificate of Institution written to *'John Alexander, clerk. Master of Arts. Greeting. We admit you to the rectory and parish church of Alderton in the County of Suffolk in the diocese of Norwich . . . In testimony of which we have affixed our Episcopal seal to these presents. Given at Heigham next Norwich on the last day of August in the year of our Lord 1648 and the seventh year of our Translation. Jos: Norvic'. Ste: Knight principal registrar.*

A document as important as this, (not forgetting that similar ones had been considered illegal by those in office at the Guildhall prior to this date *-see Chapter 4)* would not have been drawn up by the principal registrar and signed by Bishop Joseph Hall himself, ('Jos: Norvic') in some insignificant little dwelling place somewhere near Norwich. No, I feel there can be no doubt that this document was authorised and signed by bishop Hall in his palace by the river at Heigham.

Sequestration eased

In 1648 Parliament had in fact made an order which effectively discharged Bishop Hall from some elements of sequestration as regards his temporal and real estate. However, the revenues due to him as regards the Bishopric of Norwich were still denied him. Allowing him belated access to his personal estate and property at last made life a bit easier for the Halls. In these last years Bishop Hall was seen regularly in the parish of Heigham, (walking with some impediment leaning on his staff) taking monies to the poor. It must have been during these last eight years of his life that he began setting some money to one side so that it could be discharged via his will. *(See page 87)*. It is very unlikely that he could have found this money earlier in his life with his large family responsibilities. As far as we know, after the awful era of sequestration, (1643-48) he was virtually penniless. During those many occasions when his property was regularly invaded and searched, where on earth would he have adequately securely hidden the several hundred pounds he was destined to leave in his will?

The Dean and Chapter of Norwich Cathedral were officially banned on 29th May 1649 and all their lands were sold. They were to remain in dire financial straits for over a decade. The cathedral choir is certain to have been disbanded after the organ was irreverently dismantled and destroyed on a bonfire in Norwich market place in 1643. It also follows that the organist, Richard Gibbs, would have been made redundant too. No successor was appointed for seventeen-years. Organ builder Thomas Dallum was to install a new instrument in1660 at the Restoration when Richard Aylward, (a composer of note whose *'Responses'* are still sung regularly in Norwich Cathedral, amongst others) was appointed organist. Interestingly, after several new organs and 'rebuilds' along the way, the current organ, (completed in 1950) still retains some of those very old Dallum pipes.

Elizabeth Hall RIP

Joseph lost his wife Elizabeth on 27 August 1652. She was 69. They had been married for a considerable span and had certainly known some turbulent times together. In later life Joseph was to say of his wife that she was ... *a grave, virtuous matron, with whom I lived forty-nine years"*. The lettering on her monument, (sadly destroyed in enemy action April

1942) detailed below, inexplicably mentions *forty-eight* years of marriage.
Perhaps it seemed longer to Joseph! Elizabeth's memorial was erected in St
Bartholomew's church on the south wall of the nave. We do not know
precisely where in the church she was buried but, if it was adjacent to her
memorial it would point to somewhere towards the west end of the nave
and close by the south wall. Elizabeth Hall's mural tablet, (with its final
line carved as a stark warning to those perusing it) was engraved, in
English, as follows:

> ELIZABETH THE DEARE AND VERTUOUS
> CONSORT OF JOSEPH HALL B:N: WITH
> WHOM SHE COMFORTABLY LIVED
> FORTY EIGHT YEARS CHANGED
> THIS MORTALL LIFE FOR AN
> ETERNALL, AUGUST 27. 1652.
> IN THE YEAR OF HER AGE 69
> FAREWELL READER AND MIND ETERNITIE

Interestingly, she and Joseph had also chosen that final line some ten years
earlier in 1642, *(detailed in Chapter Four)* for their son Edward's
memorial brass in the cathedral Presbytery. Joseph was to use it too, (but
carved in Latin to reflect his status) for his own grave slab in 1656. It is not
unreasonable to presume that they both rather liked its austere and
cautionary warning. Was Joseph reacting to his mother's 'advice' from
beyond the grave?

During his last thirteen
years Joseph Hall acted as
assistant priest to the
Revd. John Whitefoot at
the small 15th century
church of St Bartholomew,
in the Hamlet of Heigham,
where he attended often
and sometimes preached,
the last time probably
being on 1st July 1655 – on his 81st birthday. An excerpt from this sermon
will be found on *page 84*. The adjacent picture, *(above)* dating I think from
the 1830s, depicts the north side of the church and shows the north porch,

(jutting out to the right near the base of the tower) and also the vestry built onto the same frontage towards its eastern end, complete with chimney. In the early 19th century, when the illustration above was drawn, I have discovered that land to the north of the church extended right down to the riverbank. Approaching the building from this direction held a surprise, for the churchyard itself could only be entered via a stile. Presumably the area nearest the river was pasture. (See also the entry under John Hall in *Appendix B*). During my research I was told the fascinating late 19th century tale of a bride being brought up the river from Norwich to this church for her wedding onboard a sailing Wherry. She alighted on the riverbank near to Mile Cross Bridge. From there the bridal party must have walked across the pasture and tackled that stile before getting to the church – on time, hopefully!

Victorian re-building and a special dedication

The church was originally served by a north and south porch, both positioned near the base of the tower. However, a significant adjustment to the church in 1878 saw the addition of a new north aisle plus one-hundred extra seats, increasing the sittings to three-hundred. The old north porch and vestry were removed and a robing vestry was created behind the organ chamber to the north of the sanctuary. Modifications were also made to the original nave and the tower. How fitting that this additional structure should be dedicated to Bishop Joseph Hall, who had first been buried in the church on 8th September 1656, and by all accounts on the very evening of his death, for the burial Register clearly says so. See *page 85.*

As a mark of respect for this church's former illustrious prelate, the Rector, the Revd. S. Linton laid the foundation stone, *(left)* marking the new north aisle construction in 1878. Although somewhat weathered and ravaged by the bombing of 1942, this large stone still stands today, albeit in rather splendid isolation, within the old church site. The lettering is largely indecipherable today even though I have coloured in blue several of the characters carved on it. I was only able to do this after discovering a full account of the lettering in a *'History of the Hamlet of Heigham'* written by Edward Delves and published in 1879 - when the carving was new. The legend at the time read as follows:

TO THE GLORY OF GOD, AND IN MEMORY OF BISHOP HALL, AND OF THE ENLARGEMENT AND COMPLETE RESTORATION OF THE CHURCH OF ST. BARTHOLOMEW HEIGHAM, THIS STONE WAS LAID ON THE 20TH OF APRIL AD 1878.

Although philanthropic wealthy individuals had generously donated some of the funding, sympathetic parishioners had contributed a sizeable balance and other monies were raised at a special event held in Saint Andrew's Hall, Norwich in 1877. The fund-raisers were shrewd in having the whole innovative project undertaken in memory of its worthy former priest and bishop. How wonderful that we may confidently say that the good name of Joseph Hall was seeing a creditable resurgence in the hearts and deeds of the good folk of this parish during the latter part of the 19th century.

The church reopened for worship some eight months later on 12th December 1878 – just in time for the Christmas celebrations. A new altar came into use on this special occasion. It had been generously donated to the church by the Revd. H. Howell of Drayton, who dedicated it in glowing praise to bishop Joseph Hall. A carved memorial legend ran around this table as follows:

> *Hinds Howell, clerk, M.A., Rector of Drayton, dedicated this new altar table to Almighty God. A.D. 1878, in memory of Joseph Hall DD Lord Bishop of Norwich, who died in 1656, but whose virtues and learning, as also the persecution which he endured, still linger in the hearts of English Churchmen.*

St Bartholomew's 'Blitzed' 29th April 1942

Sadly, this generous gift and the fine sentiment it so nobly bore, was to perish in the flames of that awful night in 1942. Remarkably, some items of significance survived this grim event. The safe had been blasted from its site within the Vestry wall and we understand somebody – doubtless well meaning – disastrously cut the back out whilst it and its contents were still hot. This action proved to be catastrophic, for as soon as the cooler

82

oxygenated outside air made contact with the heated contents, the parish registers stored inside burst into flames, and a prevailing strong wind scattered many of the burning pages to all parts of the smouldering ruinous site. The registers were dated 1790-1812, (burials) and another starting at 1753 contained marriage records. A transcribed micro-fiche version of these precious strewn fragments was produced and this can be inspected at the Norfolk Records Office.

The safe had also contained some items of very important silver and these were taken to the house of a local resident, a Mrs. Bream of 186 Nelson Street, for secure storage immediately after the disastrous fire in the church. Interestingly, a quick look at my *Kelly's Directory* for Norwich dated 1954 still had a Mrs. Ethel Lucy Bream listed, (as a shopkeeper) at this address. Thanks to expert advice from Nigel Bumphrey, (Norwich Diocesan Advisor for Silver) together with invaluable records copied to me by Richard Hoggett of the Norfolk and Norwich Archaeological Society, it

is now possible to say with guarded certainty what silverware items were in the ill-fated safe on the night of 29th April 1942.

This is very significant information, for some of the silverware would certainly have been used by Bishop Joseph Hall at St. Bartholomew's Church, Heigham, Norwich between ca.1646 and his death in 1656, and certainly one piece bore a 19th century dedication to him. A full and detailed listing of the silver and one surviving precious glass item is to be found at

Appendix B.

[Illustration © Norfolk County Council Library and Information Service – photograph by George Swain showing the south-west aspect of the burnt-out shell of St. Bartholomew's Church in 1953 – some eleven years after the disastrous air-raid fire]

Bishop Joseph Hall's last sermon

Joseph Hall's last extant sermon, (to which he gave the title *"Life a Sojourning")* given in this church dates from Sunday1st July 1655 – his eighty-first birthday. He took for his text 1. Peter 1.17. *"And if ye call on the Father, who without respect of persons judgeth according to every man's work, pass the time of your sojourning here in fear."* A modern translation of this passage from the Revised Standard Version of the bible reads: *And if you invoke as Father him who judges each one impartially according to his deeds, conduct yourselves with fear throughout the time of your exile.*

An extract from this final sermon belies Joseph's failing health for it is a positive affirmation of his continuing mental capacity even if the body was now so weak.

> *"It hath pleased the providence of my God so to contrive it, that this day, this very morning, [5am] fourscore years ago, I was born into this world. 'A great time since' ye are ready to say: and so indeed it seems to you, that look at it forward; but to me, that look at it past, it seems so short, that it is gone like a tale that is told, or a dream by night, and looks but like yesterday. It can be no offence for me to say that, many of you who hear me this day, are not like to see so many suns walk over your heads, as I have done. Yea, what speak I of this? There is not one of us, that can assure himself of his continuance here one day. We are all tenants at will; and, for ought we know, may be turned out of these clay cottages at an hours warning. Oh, then, what should we do, but, as wise farmers, who know the time of their lease is expiring and cannot be renewed, carefully and seasonably provide ourselves of a surer and more during tenure?"*

One wonders if Joseph was drawn to this text by its parallel with his own five years of extreme suffering, (1643-48) at the hands of his enemies. Was he connecting this with a feeling that he had indeed been 'exiled' during these years? As always with Joseph, a fascinating thought. From about this time in 1655 Joseph's health was set to rapidly decline. For many years he had suffered from a seriously painful intestinal condition known then as *stranguary* – and today diagnosed as kidney stones. By all accounts he had stoically borne this often-acute condition. Even during his infirmity he was nevertheless seen struggling round his parish every week taking money to poor women. In the final thirteen years of his life from 1643 he had still continued to write. He had at least six books published during this period. Many of his works, (certainly upwards of forty books and pamphlets in his lifetime) were so popular that they reprinted before his death.

In the last months of Joseph Hall's life, his good old friend, Dr Thomas Browne, the famous Norwich physician, writer botanist and academic, attended this very frail and dying man. Apparently Joseph unerringly foretold the precise night of his death to those administering to him, and accordingly left orders for the time and manner of his funeral, at which he desired there should *'be no pomp.'* Even the attention of a hugely respected and notable doctor could not stop the inevitable from happening, and on the evening of Friday 8th September 1656, Joseph Hall died. We are told he was laid to rest that very day, (evening) *in the chancel* of St Bartholomew's church in Heigham. The Burial Register states *'Joseph Hall, late Bishop of Norwich, was buried September 8th 1656.'* This discounts any thought that his body was placed before the altar to lie overnight in respectful peace before interment. He had asked for no pomp and that part of his wishes were fulfilled.

Did the bell toll for Bishop Hall?

George Lewis has put forward a very thought-provoking comment on the bishop's passing in his biography *'A life of Joseph Hall DD'*, (London 1886). Lewis promotes the likelihood that Joseph would have sanctioned the tolling of a bell at St. Bartholomew's as he drew towards his end. Apparently Joseph generally thought such observance to be most fitting, so that all living close by could pray for the departing soul and plead for mercy as it passed from this life to immortal glory. I have found no record that the church bell tolled in this fashion at Joseph's passing - but that does not rule out the possibility that it did. If a bell was heard it was almost certainly one of the two that came crashing down from the church tower into the baptistry during the raging fire on that terrible night in April 1942.

It's not difficult to imagine that a message was taken the short distance from the palace to the church before dusk on the evening he died. The verger or sexton could therefore toll the bell until such time as was

85

appropriate to cease. Even during his failing grip on life Joseph would have been immensely strengthened in spirit on hearing the sonorous tone of the bell sounding from the tower of the little church he loved so well. Perhaps the evening of 8th September 1656 was mild enough for a window to be opened so as to allow the dying bishop to hear this friendly and comforting sound. In 1656 there would have been no noise pollution and only open ground separated the two fairly adjacent buildings.

A posthumous collection of Joseph Hall's works was published four years after his death in 1660, under the title of *'The Shaking of the Olive Tree'*. Included within this book I found what I believe to be the very first published version of his famous *'Hard Measure'* account of the iconoclastic damage perpetrated in Norwich Cathedral during 1643 – *see Chapter Four*. Most commentators have typically assigned a much later date for its publication - 1700 being typical. Joseph actually dated the completion of this iconic work as 29th May 1647. The memory of the sad events four years prior to this would of course still be all too painfully clear to Joseph.

'The Shaking of the Olive Tree' has an anonymous Preface and, even though it has been regularly quoted by other writers, the identity of its author has lain unresolved down the centuries. However, I'm certain my research has at last resolved this mystery. Upon reading the *Preface* my eye was instantly drawn to one particular line, which I recalled seeing elsewhere in my researches. The line in question is printed below in *bold type*. The common link between its double uses is, I am certain, a pointer to the anonymous *Preface* at the beginning of *The Shaking of the Olive Tree* being unquestionably the work of the Revd. John Whitefoot, who presided at the bishop's funeral service at St Peter Mancroft Church, Norwich on 30th September 1656. In the *Preface* is a description of Bishop Hall's final moments in the following touching sentences:

> *"Afflictions of the body, (stones and stranguary) persued him to death but could not hinder his activities in both Press and Pulpit. His intellect and senses continued strong and fresh to the last. His head was Gold and his heart refined Silver when the rest of his body was clay. He set aside one day per week for fasting and humiliation with his Family. The tempestuous storm, which blew him off course, battered his vessel and tore his sails, did but drive*

him to the quiet haven where he was content to be. [His palace and church at Heigham.] *After many holy prayers, exhortations, and discourses,* **he roused up his dying Spirits, to a heavenly Confession of his Faith** *which, before he could finish, his speech failed. After some strugglings of nature, with the agonies of death, he quietly, gradually, gave up his last breath".*

Compare the above extract from *The Shaking of the Olive Tree* with the excerpt from the sermon preached by Revd. John Whitefoot at St. Peter Mancroft Church, Norwich, on 30th September 1656, which will be found below under *Joseph Hall's Memorial Service.*

The will of Bishop Joseph Hall

Signed on 21st July 1654 with a short Memorandum added 28th April 1656, just over four months before his death.

In the name of God, Amen. "I Joseph Hall, Doctor of Divinity (not worthy to be called Bishop of Norwich), considering the certainty of death and the great uncertainty of life, have thought much in the state of my wonted health to make my last Will and testament in manner following. First I bequeath my soule into the hands of my Faithful Creator and Redeemer, not doubting but that he will receive it to mercy and crowne it with glorye. My body I leave to be interred without funerall pompe, at the discretion of my executor, with this only monition, that I do not hold God's house a meet repositorie for the dead bodyes of the greatest Saints.
My house and grounds in the City of Exeter I give my eldest sonne Robt Hall Dr of Divinity and his heires for ever. Moreover to my sonne Joseph I give and bequeath all that freeland with the appurtenances which I have in Much Bentley in the County of Essex with the edifices thereto belonging. And whereas I am informed that the custome of that manor is such that the Coppyhold lands except they be formerly Surrendered into the hands of the Tenants to other uses, Do in course descend upon the youngest sonne, my Will is that my sonne Samuel (upon whom it will fall) doe speedily surrender that Copyhold and the Tenements thereto belonging to the use and behoof of my Sd Sonne Joseph, and his heires for ever.

Also to my sonne George I give and bequeath all that terme and remainder of yeares which I have in the Dwelling-house wherein I now remain, and the groundes thereto belonging, with all the appurts to be entered upon by him within 3 months after my decease.

To my Sonne Samuel Hall, whoe is yet only of all my Sonnes blessed with any issue, I will and do give and bequeath all those my lands and tenements with their appurtanences, situate, lying and being in the parish of Totnesse in the County of Devon. My three sonnes, I thanke Gode I have lived to see learned, judicious and painfull divines.

To my Sonne in Law, Mr. Dr. Peterson, Deane of Exeter, I give that curious flappe which was given me by Mr. Rawlins, and one faire gilt bowle with cover, for a remembrance of my deare affection to him,

To my grandchild Elizabeth Hall I give £300. To my grandchild Mary Hall I give £100. I doe make and ordaine my Sonne Samuel Hall my full, lawfull and sole executor, not doubtinge of his true fidelity therein; and do desire and appoint my beloved Sonne in Law Gascoigne Weld, and my loving friend and neighbour Mr. George Bayfield, to be overseers thereof, giving to my Sd Sonne my Golden Medall which was given me by Mrs. Goodwin; and to Mr. Bayfield one piece of plate, viz., one Silver Tankard.

And that this is my last will and testament I doe publish and declare, suscribinge the same and affixing my seale Manuell, this 21st day of July, in the Year of our Lord God 1654."

Jos. Hall B.N.

Published, signed, and sealed in the presence of us, Geo. Bayfield, Peregrine Pond, Edmond Camplin, Margaret Hatley, Athanasius Ferrer, John Reeve.

That all the words inserted or altered in the severall places of this will are written and done by my owne hand, and are by me accordingly published as part of my will Aprill 28, 1656. In the presence of Peregrine Pond, Margaret Hatley, Edmond Camplin.

Jos. Hall, B.N.

In addition to the above the following will extracts to be found at Norfolk Records Office are also of interest. **Joseph Hall jnr**, (the only layman amongst his surviving sons) received all lands and tenements in Essex but had to forego this right by surrendering the property and land to his brother *Samuel Hall*. *George Hall* also received all lands and tenements in Mulbarton near Norwich in addition to his rights to the Palace at Heigham. Each of these three sons also received £200. *Samuel Hall*, the youngest surviving son, *"who is yet only of all my sons blessed with any issue"* was chosen as the sole executor of the estates. He was also given the lands and tenements at Totnes in Devon, and the Bishop's library – except that **Robert** and **George** *"whom I know to be well provided in that kind"* were to have twenty books between them. Joseph Hall's notes and sermons were to be divided between **Robert** and **George**, the rest of his 'paper-books' [I judge this term to mean any unbound volumes] were left to **Samuel** and were not to be *"meddled with or disposed without the joint consent of my said 3 sons whom I thank God I have lived to see learned, judicious and painful divines"*.

The sons were enjoined "upon the blessing of a father*"* not to alienate the lands and tenements bequeathed to them *"except they be necessitated by the times or the exingencies of their own particular estate, for the true reality of which necessity I lay weight on their conscience of the Lord"*. If they were to die without male issue, (Samuel's children were both girls) they were instructed to leave these lands and tenements to the next brother or to his issue, [presumably males first] or to the issue of their sister *Mrs. Weld. [Ann Hall]*. Joseph's son-in-law, **Gascoigne Weld**, and his loving friend and neighbour, **Mr George Bayfield**, were to be the overseers.

There were also bequests of plate to Weld, Bayfield and to Dr Peterson, the Dean of Exeter, who had married the bishop's eldest daughter Elizabeth, who was now dead without leaving issue. *"My golden medal, which was given me by the States of the Netherlands for my applause at the Synod of Dort"* was to be given to any male issue of his sons, and in default of such issue it was to go to *Joseph Weld* who was Joseph senior's only male grandchild. *(See also pages 35 and 36)*. There were also bequests to several servants. The poor of Heigham received £10; his birthplace, Ashby-de-la-Zouch was left £30, and the City of Norwich also received £30.

I have not been able to discover any details about the gold medal given to him by Mrs. Goodwin – who we may assume to be the same good soul who generously bought all Bishop Hall's confiscated belongings in 1643, prior to returning them to him. See *Chapter Four*. Also unresolved is a description of 'that curious flappe' (originally gifted to Bishop Hall by a Mr Rawlins) given by bishop Joseph to his son-in-law Dr William Peterson. I think we must assume that Joseph was describing a piece of silver that was both ornate and attractively shaped.

Joseph Hall's Memorial Service

Prior to his death Joseph had reluctantly given his consent for a memorial sermon to be preached in his honour on a separate occasion after the private funeral service, which we must assume was held in St. Bartholomew's Church shortly after his death on 8th September 1656. I have not been able to establish exactly when his funeral service was conducted or indeed who was there. However, the special memorial service we know a deal more about. It was held in St. Peter Mancroft Church, Norwich on 30th September 1656 and included a grand valedictory sermon. Perhaps the eminent venue was chosen as a fitting place for its civic importance, after the cathedral, (obviously out of the question) and for its capacity to potentially house a significantly large congregation. The Revd. John Whitefoot MA, Rector of St. Bartholomew's Church, himself instituted by Bishop Hall in 1652, gave a long and wonderfully warm tribute to his late honoured friend. Interestingly, the sermon was dedicated to Joseph's eldest son, Robert, (the Treasurer at Exeter Cathedral) whom we must assume was in attendance with his wife Rebecca.

Later that year the sermon was available to purchase from a London publisher in 8vo [ca. A5] size for 5/- and Joseph would have undoubtedly been delighted to have known this for he had often published his sermons and speeches. Within its pages we find the following emotional account of the very private and personal last moments of Joseph's life. All his great sufferings and emotional distresses at the hands of his enemies were now ended and, at the last, in a moment of faltering sweet bliss, he was finally allowed to go to his rest. This is part of what Revd. John Whitefoot had to say about his old friend Joseph's death.

> *"After his prevailing infirmities had wasted all the strengths of nature, and the arts of his learned and excellent physician, Dr Browne of Norwich, (to whom, under God, we and the whole Church are ingaged for many years preserving his life and blessing to us) – after his fatherly reception of many persons of honour,*

*learning, and piety, who came to crave his dying prayers and benedictions – **he roused up his dying spirits, to a heavenly confession of his faith** . . . Sure we do all well to help to embalm his name, especially since we may do it at his own cost, for he hath provided the spices in his life. When he lived, his lips dropped myrrh, and his pen the oil of calamus and cinnamon; the smell whereof hath filled the house of God with such perfume, as I hope this age, as ill-scented as it is, will never wear out".*

Joseph's physician Dr Thomas Brown, mentioned earlier, was in attendance at the funeral itself in St. Bartholomew's Church sometime earlier in September 1656. He left the following comment on that rather precious occasion. I strongly suspect however that it was a retrospective account of the event because the *monument* mentioned is unlikely to have been in place at the actual time of the funeral service. On the other hand, according to those able to view and assess it before its destruction in April 1942, it was generally thought to have been poorly rendered. So was it hastily and badly executed? We simply do not know.

"My honoured friend Bishop Joseph Hall, Dean of Worcester, and Bishop of Exeter, was buried at Heigham, where he hath his monument, who in the Rebellious time, when the Revenues of the church were alienated, retired unto that suburban parish, and there ended his days: being above fourscore years of age. A person of singular humility, patience and piety: his own works are the best monument, and character of himself, which was also very lively drawn in his excellent funeral sermon preached by my learned friend Mr John Whitefoot, Rector of Heigham".

An obvious question arises from reading this account. Why doesn't Dr Browne accord his old friend the title of Bishop of Norwich? There could be three reasons for this. Firstly, it was obvious and didn't need stating, or, secondly, it was omitted in the belief that he had lost this title when so cruelly ejected from the cathedral more than ten years previously. A third, and more intriguing possibility, is that Dr Browne duly acknowledged and reflected in this funeral service memoir, that Joseph Hall had stated clearly in his will that he was not considered *worthy* of the title of Bishop of Norwich. The learned Doctor may well have been perpetuating his old friend's sad comment by ignoring this ecclesiastical title. It was of course true that Joseph Hall had been denied some of his due incomes as a bishop and unjustly ousted from office. However, since nobody officially succeeded him until Bishop Reynolds in 1661, I would certainly argue that he was still the title-holder up to his death in 1656.

Bishop Hall's Monument

The monument, to which Dr Browne alludes, was a very ornate mural carving and was placed on the south wall inside the church, by the chancel. We have an excellently detailed description of this from information noted by John Jones when writing his book: *'Bishop Hall, His Life and Times'* published in 1826 by L.B. Seeley & Sons, London. Note his comment on the workmanship.

> *"Mural Monument: placed directly above the grave on the south wall, was of stone intermixed with black marble and of rather coarse workmanship. The pediment, in which it finished, is surmounted with a mitre in relief, and the arms of Hall singly (Sable 3 Talbots' heads erased Arg.) are under the pediment. The principal feature of the monument is the figure of a skeleton executed in gilding on an arch-headed black marble tablet, which occupies the whole space from the pediment to a plinth at the bottom. The figure holds in its right hand a scroll with a seal attached to it, inscribed:*

Debemus Morti Nos Nostraque:
[We and all our possessions are condemned at our death]
And in its left hand another scroll, from which a seal has been torn, inscribed:
Persolvit et quietus est.
[His life is completed and he is now at rest]

On the tablet between the legs of the figure is engraved:

OBIT 8 SEPTEM. ANO
AERÆ CHRISTIANÆ 1656 AEA
SUAE 82.
*[HE DIED 8TH SEPTEMBER IN THE YEAR
OF CHRIST 1656 AND*

On the plinth of the black marble is engraved:

> JOSEPHUS HALLUS OLIM HUILIS
> ECCLESIÆ SERVUS
> *[JOSEPH HALL ONCE A HUMBLE SERVANT*
> *OF THE CHURCH]*

The above reference to the mural monument being placed on the south wall of the church *immediately above* the grave or vault is very interesting. This would clearly suggest that the mortal remains of Joseph Hall were not buried where the ledger slab dedicated to him could later be found, i.e. in the central aisle before the chancel step. It would seem that he was actually buried in a vault at the base of the south inside wall. Another point of contention is the instruction left in his will.

Bishop Hall's Monument.

"In the name of God, Amen. I Joseph Hall, D.D. not worthy to be called Bishop of Norwich, etc. First I bequeath my soul etc. My body I leave to be <u>interred</u>, without any funeral pomp, at the descretion of my Executors; with the only monition, that I do not hold God's house a meet repository for the dead bodies of the greatest saints".

[Illustration of Bishop Joseph Hall's Monument ca. 1910. Courtesy of Norfolk Records Office]

You have to feel a crushing compassion for the wounded soul who wrote that he was considered unworthy to be called bishop of Norwich. Neither is it difficult to sense from these words the pain he had to bear during his wilful ejection from office in 1643. His level of hurt was such that he wanted to have this statement included in this, his final document. Is there not also a quiet, almost *satirical* mocking reserved for his previous adversaries within this apparently self-deprecating sentence? I think so.

His ardent wish to be buried without the confines of a church building has already been fully covered in *Chapter Three* under *Bishop Hall's grave pronouncement*. It is surprising therefore that he gave a bit of latitude over this matter to his Executors. In their judgement they decided not to use the churchyard and we can perhaps understand why. It seems likely that Joseph's health – already fragile - noticeably deteriorated during a period of days before his death. This being so, would it not be likely that those responsible for his final resting place, would have made some anticipatory arrangements? It would seem that his body was placed in a vault space which was in all probability opened up and prepared for him in the days leading to his demise. Further, if it *is* true that his body was laid to rest in a vault on the evening of the very day of his death, the fact that the burial site was already prepared for would preclude the necessity of hurried burial site provision. However, a second consideration may also have weighed on the minds of Joseph's Executors.

The tumultuous events and resultant instability in the country, (and in Bishop Hall's own life from 1641) had led some notable families to conclude that even after burial, the security of their loved-one's remains could not be guaranteed against grave violation by extreme vengeance-seeking fanatics. Desecration of graves in churches and cathedrals up and down the country had certainly taken place as we know from the gross acts of vandalism perpetrated in Norwich Cathedral in 1643, covered in *Chapter Four*. Even the tomb of the cathedral's founder, Bishop Herbert de Losinga, was wrecked in front of the high altar. Although Joseph Hall had been allowed to lead a relatively secluded life after the mid 1640s it could nevertheless have occurred to his family and Executors that a strong and secure resting place in a sealed stone vault held less risk of sacrilege than an obviously freshly dug burial pit in the churchyard. His death in September 1656 was still some four years before stability was restored by the accession of King Charles II in 1660. In 1656, after the bloody struggles of the Civil War had led to the imposition of The Commonwealth, nobody was remotely able to predict when life under a monarch might resume again. Burial of his body, without delay, in a sealed vault would almost certainly preclude its violation – if that was a major concern to Joseph's family. Whatever the controversy about the vault we know that there was a grave slab positioned above it and we know that it contained the following legend:

INDULVE JOSEPHI HALL
OLIM NORVICENSIS
ECCLESIÆ SERVI
REPOSITÆ 8° DIE MENSIS
SEPTEMBRIS ANNO DOMINI
1656 ÆTATIS SUÆ
ANNO 82°
VALE LECTOR ET
ÆTERNITATI
PROSPICE
[HERE LIE THE REMAINS OF JOSEPH HALL
WHO IN RECENT TIMES WAS A SERVANT OF THE CHURCH IN
NORWICH. HE FELL TO REST THE 8TH DAY OF
SEPTEMBER IN THE YEAR OF OUR LORD
1656 IN HIS
82ND YEAR
TAKE CARE READER AND
BE MINDFUL OF ETERNITY]

At a later date it is recorded that the black marble grave slab was removed to make way for the addition of an extra pew. One imagines that this was a remedy showing some respect for the famous prelate, so as not to obliterate his memorial in the paving by the south inner wall. We are told that the slab was in fact repositioned in the central chancel aisle, adjacent to the step leading into the sanctuary. However, this perfectly reasonable action has inevitably led to confusion in later decades as to precisely where the body was originally buried. I think it unlikely that the mortal remains would have been disturbed, so probably only the stone floor slab was moved from above the burial vault into the central aisle before the altar. See Appendix A - *John Hall* for further references to this grave slab.

The repositioning of the slab can be dated to ca. 1820. A very interesting event followed in 1823, for, whilst excavation work was in hand nearby for the burial of a former priest's widow, a substantial vault was detected exactly where the black marble slab had formerly been sited. From this evidence can we say in all probability that the original burial site of Bishop Hall's body was in the vault below the south wall of the chancel area?

Saint Bartholomew's Church Tower, Heigham, Norwich
photographed by the Author in October 2011. It stands in splendid
isolation within a landscaped area, which was formerly its churchyard
until 1975, when it was developed into a local amenities park. The site
is well worth visiting to view the outline structure pattern of the
demolished parish church. It can be entered via Waterworks Road or
alternatively from Nelson Street – through St. Bartholomew's Close.

CHAPTER SIX

Bishop Joseph Hall's final resting place - and an amazing discovery.

To all intents and purposes there should be no need for this chapter to exist, but delving into the Hall family has constantly surprised me with its unanticipated revelations and outcomes. In this concluding chapter we discover that in 1975, some 319 years after his death, Joseph Hall was destined to be the recipient of a final and thoroughly appropriate act of benevolent kindness. However, before revealing the detail of this amazing event, it is necessary to review a sad portion of history relating to Joseph Hall's last church and his original resting place.

As previously stated elsewhere, during the night of the 29th of April 1942 St Bartholomew's church was destroyed by enemy action. By cruel irony bishop Hall's old palace nearby was also gutted during the same air raid and no doubt both structures perished within seconds of each other by incendiary bombs from the same enemy aircraft. The two pictures above are almost unbelievably of the same view inside the church looking west. The first, (left) was taken in 1938 by the late George Plunkett who has left Norwich a fine photographic resource and website, which is altruistically managed by his generous son Jonathan. The second picture, (right) comes from Norfolk County Council's Library and Information archive, and shows in horrific detail the devastation inflicted on the church by enemy action that night in 1942. The badly damaged church building, apart from the tower, was eventually cleared away in the 1950s. Prior to this in 1945 an extensive survey was undertaken at this site by a team from Norfolk Archaeology. Today, the original layout of the church can be deduced from the helpful previous wall positions indicated by markers set into the ground. However, I have found that these extant groundwork footings are not fully reliable when compared with pre-war 20th century photographic evidence, and 19th century church layout measurements. However, notwithstanding this the site, *(pictured on page 96 in October 2011)* is well worth a visit as it still retains a curious and beguiling attraction. One can still sense that its former atmospheres of holiness still linger there.

Although Joseph's mortal remains may well have lain slumbering all those years in the chancel area of this charming little church this was not to be the end of his influence within our current era, for we may say that his story was merely put 'on hold' in 1656. Just a few decades after the war-ravaged demise of St. Bartholomew's Church, another bishop's heart was to be so touched and moved by Joseph's plight in life, that it brought forth a final wonderfully warm gesture of reconciliation for bishop Joseph Hall.

The quest to find Bishop Hall's final resting place!

In 1975 the local council determined to redevelop the graveyard at St Bartholomew's by landscaping it into a leisure area with associated children's play park. After contacting The Church Commissioner's (TCC) in London I discovered that they had in that year notified the parish of their intention to declare the church ruins as 'redundant'. After due process, and there being no local reaction to contest this proposed action, TCC sanctioned the ruins being so declared on 1st June 1975, *(TCC - Pastoral and Closed Division - Section 28)*. A further order granted 'upkeep ownership' of the remaining tower structure and church site to Norwich City Council on 27th October 1976, by officially declaring that the extant church tower be classed hereafter as a 'monument'. *(TCC – Pastoral and Closed Division - Section 50)*.

Meanwhile, prior to this redevelopment, the then Bishop of Norwich, (the Rt. Revd. Maurice Wood) asked the then Archdeacon of Norwich, (the Ven. Timothy Dudley-Smith) to obtain a Faculty which would allow for the mortal remains of Bishop Joseph Hall to be removed from the St.

Bartholomew's site for re-interment in the Cloister Garth at Norwich Cathedral. Faculty 0084/74 was duly granted on 13th December 1974 to approve this somewhat unique action. (See *Appendix C* for full details of the relevant correspondence). The late Bishop Wood was on record as declaring that he thought merely placing protective railings around Bishop Hall's important grave would not be sufficient security to keep it from harm. The stone slab over the grave was apparently already badly cracked. Sadly, its whereabouts is currently unknown. It would be satisfying to find it sometime.

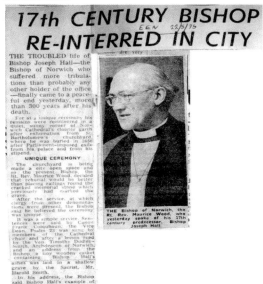

Within a few weeks of starting my investigations Jonathan Plunkett, (son of the late noted Norwich photographer George Plunkett) sent me a copy, *(as pictured left)* of a Press cutting from his father's extensive archive. It was from the Norwich Evening News of 22nd May 1975 and it recorded the re-burial ceremony of the previous day held in the Garth of Norwich Cathedral cloisters. This was a great step forward. It mentioned that Bishop Joseph Hall's remains were placed in a small casket and, during a short but poignant open-air service, the then Cathedral Sacrist, Mr Harold Smith, placed the bishop's remains in a shallow grave *'in a quiet sunny corner of Norwich Cathedral's Cloister Garth'*. Frustratingly, it did not precisely pin-point the actual corner used!

Upon enquiry I was told that, until 1978 it was not customary to note the precise site of modern burials in the Garth. I couldn't help thinking it was a shame that such an important individual's burial site was not noted. After all, Bishop Maurice Wood had gone to a good deal of trouble to do the right thing by the formerly oppressed bishop. Having been very moved by the extraordinary suffering of bishop Joseph Hall, not to mention his great importance within the history of Norwich, I resolved to somehow locate his final resting place. Enquiries to find the 'missing' bishop started in early 2010. Little did I know this particular quest would absorb me for almost a year before its extraordinary conclusion would be revealed to me.

Many interviews and countless 'phone calls were conducted with people I thought might have useful information. Sadly, all to no avail. It didn't help that many of those who attended that Garth ceremony on 21st May 1975 were now deceased. Sadly the emerging lack of evidence began to suggest that all this investigative enterprise was frustratingly just a few years too late – or was it?

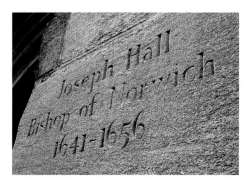

On a bleak rainy day, when adjourning to the Refectory for hot drinks might have made more sense than a finger-tip search of the cloister Garth area, Cathedral Guide colleague, Anne May 'discovered' a Joseph Hall memorial stone, *(left)* whose existence, (carved into a buttress in the SW corner of the cloister Garth) was hitherto surprisingly unknown. It was easy to now conclude the likelihood that this cloister area was that enigmatic *'sunny corner'* referred to in the Evening News press cutting. Here was potentially exciting information. The 'cold-case' began to warm up. One thing leads to another and the site of this discovery suddenly made sense, for I realised that fairly adjacent to the memorial buttress is the grave of bishop John Sheepshanks who was bishop of Norwich 1893-1910. He died in 1912. The logic of picking this area for bishop Hall now made complete sense – it was probably the 'Bishop's corner' in the mind of Bishop Wood. It's easy when you have the advantage of knowing what you're looking for! After many more weeks of mostly fruitless research the pivotal break-through was made when I fortuitously decided to check with the local Press to see if the 1975 reporter's original notes were still available. It also occurred to me that it would make sense whilst I was about it to ask if any photographs had been taken on the day in question.

I must digress here a moment and explain that the photograph of bishop Wood, which was included in the 22nd May 1975 Evening News article featured above, had not in fact been of any help with the research, for it had been taken some time before and was a 'file' image of the bishop. At an earlier 'clutching at straws' stage of my investigations I'd had the notion that the architecture photographed behind the bishop might prove exactly in which *'sunny corner'* the burial had taken place, for the initiated will know that the design of the cloister stonework falls into three eras of Gothic workmanship, making it feasible to precisely match the extant structure against features in the photograph. Sadly, this theory now had to be ruled out.

To resume - I persisted with email enquiries of Archant and was staggered to get a very prompt reply, which said that a search of the Evening News picture archive had indeed turned up about twenty pictures taken on 21st May 1975 . . . *and some covered the reburial event in question.* A joyous moment indeed! I was offered sight of a 'proof quality' copy of all the pictures – and naturally accepted. Waiting forty-eight hours for the pictures to come through my letter-box was agonising.

On 29th January 2011 the pictures I ordered from the Evening News office duly arrived and solved the mystery beyond any doubt, for there, amongst the photographs was one that showed Bishop Hall's casket being carefully placed into a shallow grave, (a few feet from the buttress containing the memorial stone in fact) by the then Sacrist, the late Harold Smith. The somewhat stressful twelve-month investigation into this intriguing aspect of Joseph Hall's story was over. I have to admit to it being a rather emotional moment. Within a short time I had taken the news to the current Sacrist, Roger Lee, and he has now plotted the precise position on the Garth burials master grid.

1975 reburial witness comes forward

As revealed earlier, Bishop Hall said on many occasions that he did not particularly hold with burials inside churches "not even for the greatest of Saints" and we know also, for whatever reason, that his wishes were not carried out. However, we now have the great comfort of knowing that the remains of this fine and honourable man are now not only reunited with his last cathedral, but that they are also resting, (as he wished) in a wonderful and holy open space "under God's heavenly vault" – as he had put it once. At long last we now also know precisely where! Typically, however, this was not to be the end of the story. I had made a commitment in October 2010 to give a public talk sometime about my Joseph Hall research. This was eventually presented in Norwich Cathedral Library on 17th May 2011. The event attracted a very large attendance and one person in the audience had a considerable surprise in store for me.

A few days prior to my talk the Features Editor at The Evening News in Norwich, (Derek James) had printed two fulsome accounts of my research into bishop Hall and had publicised my forthcoming talk. One particular reader, Mr Rex Hancy, decided to attend for he didn't just find the reburial of bishop Hall interesting – he had actually been there on that day in May 1975 and had witnessed the whole spectacle, (under rather amazing circumstances) and was anxious to pass on his recollections to me some thirty-six years later! In 1975 Mr Hancy had been a teacher at Thorpe Hamlet Middle School in Norwich and he had often taken selected pupils out on expeditions to explore local places of interest. Norwich Cathedral was a regular venue, which explains how he and a dozen hand-picked children happened to be in the cathedral cloisters on 21st May 1975. However, none of the party expected that the Bishop of Norwich, (The Rt. Revd. Maurice Wood) crook in hand and dressed in all his finery would make a bee-line for their group and address them.

He informed the pupils and their teacher that he was the Bishop of Norwich and that he was about to bury another bishop – not a statement you'd expect to hear that often! He went on to explain that he had a few clergy on hand to assist him and that a small number from the ranks of the cathedral choristers were also in attendance – but he had no congregation. Would they like to be that special group of witnesses? Of course they would, and Mr Hancy recalls that they were rather awestruck by the whole situation. The bishop had confided in Mr Hancy that not much of the ancient bishop had been retrieved from his earlier resting place, but what there was had been placed into a small casket ready for the reburial that day.

As the children had been asked to stand in the middle of the lawned Garth area in order to see clearly all that was happening, (where the Labyrinth is now situated) it unfortunately placed them just outside the right hand range of the official photographer's camera lens, so very sadly there is no official photographic record of the very important duty they fulfilled that special day.

Even though it would have been wonderful to have had this 21st May 1975 eye-witness account earlier when my investigation work had apparently stalled, I couldn't resist the distinct feeling that the spirit of Joseph Hall had somehow contrived to intervene and so allow this last act to be played out in such a surprising and revelatory manner.

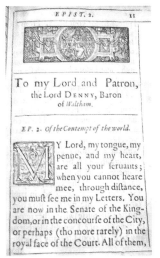

The Title Page of one of Joseph Hall's famous *Epistles*. This one is dedicated to his Patron Lord Denny of Waltham. *See Chapter Three.*

APPENDIX A

A full listing of the children of Joseph and Elizabeth Hall, including considerable detail hitherto unpublished. In his lifetime Bishop Joseph Hall was thought to have shown his sons exceptional patronage. The evidence in the following biographies does certainly point to them benefiting rather well in their receipt of generous benefices. In the records the phrase *'on mandate of the bishop'* accompanies many of his sons' appointments. To have a balanced view we must realise that nepotistic favours were rather common at Exeter *before* Joseph Hall was installed as the fortieth bishop of that diocese. When he arrived at Exeter Joseph found that the Chapter of nine canons included two brothers, (the Cottons) "besides their cousins." Let's just say that Joseph was a generous father who, like any other, simply wanted his sons to have good prospects.

Robert Hall
(1605-1667)

The eldest son, Robert, was baptised at Hawstead on 26th December 1605 – by his father one presumes. It is very likely that he was named after Joseph's patron Sir Robert Drury. Such a humble gesture would no doubt be as well received as intended. When aged twenty-three the Dean and Chapter of Exeter Cathedral awarded him a Grant on 29th March 1628 – barely four months after his father was appointed bishop! The Chapter records give Robert's status as *'a Fellow of Exeter College, Oxford'* and that he was *'located'* at Oxford. The entry is also endorsed *'decimus tertius socius'* which I assume indicates he was the thirteenth fellow so supported? I suppose we might well wonder why *Robert* was sent to Exeter College, Oxford vice Emmanuel College, Cambridge, where his father had been educated. Further delving into the Dean and Chapter records at Exeter Cathedral revealed that Walter de Stapledon had founded Exeter College in 1314. Later, in 1587, Emmanuel College, (founded by Sir Walter Mildmay) was declared a 'sister' foundation, thus establishing an interconnecting relationship between the two establishments.

The same Chapter records state that Robert was appointed a Canon of Exeter Cathedral on 21st April 1629 followed soon after by his installation as Treasurer on 17th July 1629. According to the Chapter records both positions came his way 'on mandate of Bishop Hall' and less than two years after Joseph's election as Bishop of Exeter on 5th November 1627. Robert Hall was later installed as Archdeacon of Cornwall 'by mandate of Bishop Hall' on 20th August 1633. He was to resign this post on 8th October 1641. Had he sensed a whiff of the widespread Dean and Chapter suspensions yet to be enforced up and down the land by order of Parliament from 1641 until the Restoration in 1660? If so it could have been a shrewd move by Robert to step back from the public profile of being Archdeacon of Cornwall whilst still maintaining his position as treasurer at Exeter Cathedral. We know he held this latter post until his death in 1667, and his memorial in Exeter Cathedral, (below) endorses this. In the volatile year of 1641 his father had, (doubtless unwittingly) brought all his sons' appointments under review when he was absurdly arrested for Treason in December of that year. (See *Chapter Four* for the details of that extraordinary event).

The Dean and Chapter records at Exeter contain an inexplicable entry for the year 1643 where it states that: *Mr Hall admitted a canon residentiary 23rd September 1643 on commendation of Charles I. Hall is archdeacon of Cornwall.* How strange that the title 'Mr' had been used and that it declared that 'Mr Hall' was archdeacon of Cornwall when we know that Robert, (if indeed he is the individual implied in the record) had 'resigned' in 1641. It is not easy to ascribe this 'phantom appointment' to any of Joseph's sons.

Local legend in Exeter has it that the year of Oliver Cromwell's death in 1658 saw an attempt by the City Chamber to remove the ancient, (1313) Bishops' Throne from the cathedral. However, the resistant will of Treasurer Robert Hall saw the priceless object saved. It should be stated that this extant throne is no ordinary object for it stands some 67 feet tall and its creation is arguably one of the finest feats of 14th century Gothic carpentry to be seen anywhere in Europe.

There is a curiously worded memorial to Robert Hall in Exeter Cathedral. Translated by Parker in *Reading Latin Epitaphs* it reads:

> *Here lies Robert Hall,*
> *eldest son of the distinguished Bishop Joseph Hall,*
> *eloquent Doctor of Holy Theology. In his lifetime he was*
> *Treasurer of this church, now he is dead, he is a treasure.*
> *Living, dead, in residence here. He died on 29th May 1667*
> *aged 61.*

Robert married Rebecca, the fourth daughter and co-heiress of Richard Regnell of Creedy-Widger, Devon. Rebecca died 28th May 1664 also aged 61 years. She and Robert had no children.

Joseph Hall
(1607-1669)

The second son was doubtless named after his father, with whom he can obviously be easily confused when researching. Joseph was the only son who did not seek holy orders, although he did hold a significant position concurrent with his father's appointment as Bishop of Exeter between 1627 and 1641. Joseph was installed as *Register of the Bishop of Exeter's Consistory Court* in November 1631. His grave slab in the second bay of the south Quire aisle gives his title as 'REGISTRARIUS PRINCIPALIS HUJUS DIOCAESIOS' – *Principal Registrar of this Diocese.* The extensive archive records at Exeter Cathedral, (excellently maintained by their Archivist, Miss Ellie Jones) clearly states that Bishop Joseph Hall granted his son Joseph the lease of a manor house at Peter Hayes near Exeter from 1631 to coincide with Joseph's installation as Principal Registrar. The lease was confirmed subsequently in 1632, 1634, 1637, 1638 and 1640. Joseph was bequeathed the land and appurtenances that his father owned in Much Bentley, Essex, in precedence over the youngest son, Samuel, who ordinarily would have inherited it by right of a local custom. This could be the reason Samuel contested the will of his brother George. See Bishop Hall's will in *Chapter Five* for more detail. Joseph never married and he died on 25th March 1669 aged 61 years His memorial grave slab is in Latin and translates as follows:

HERE LIES JOSEPH HALL
ESQUIRE SON OF THE REVEREND
LORD JOSEPH ONCE BISHOP OF EXETER

AND PRINCIPAL REGISTRAR
OF THIS DIOCESE WHO
DIED THE 25TH DAY OF MARCH
1669 AGED 61

Beneath the grave slab lettering is an incised shield bearing the Coat of Arms granted to his father in 1631viz: arms, *(sable) three talbots heads erased, (argent) collared, (gules).*

Elizabeth Hall
(1610-1651)

Elizabeth was born at Hawstead and, being the first-born daughter was therefore undoubtedly named after her mother. On 28th July 1629 aged 19, (and just two years after her father had been appointed Bishop of Exeter) she married Dr. William Peterson DD, the newly-appointed Dean of Exeter. They had no children. Elizabeth died on 8th July 1651 aged 41and is buried at Stoke Canon in Devon. Dr. Peterson received a bequest of silver plate from Joseph Hall's will. Dr Peterson died on 6th December 1661 aged 74. He is also buried at Stoke Canon in Devon.

George Hall
(1612-1668)

The ill-fated third son, George, was very likely named after his maternal grand father. He was baptised 24th August 1613 at Waltham, Essex and was educated at Exeter College, Oxford from1628. His brothers Robert, John and Edward were also sent to the same college. He attained his BA in 1631 and MA in 1634. He was a fellow from 1632 until his resignation in June 1638. In October 1637 he was appointed vicar of Menheniot in Cornwall. During the English Civil War he was not only sequestered from this living and removed from the archdeaconry, but also had a request to open a school forbidden. Parliament, however, allowed George and his wife, (Gertrude) compensation. In November 1651 he was *'chosen'* as the minister of St.

Bartholomew's-by-the-Exchange in London. Three years later on 5th November 1654 the vestry elected him Rector. However, this was not a popular move and the 'keepers of the great seal', (to whom the living belonged) disallowed him from that post. The church no longer exists. He became the Rector of Berwick in Sussex and of St. Botolph, Aldersgate, London, 1654-55. At the Restoration he became a Chaplain to King Charles II and was made Doctor of Divinity becoming the Bishop of Chester on 24th April 1662, with his installation there on 11th May the same year.

George Hall was the generous donor of an outstanding 17th Century gold cup and cover, (*pictured left and overleaf*) to his old college, Exeter, in Oxford in 1669. It is an object of rare beauty and arguably a piece of national significance for this pot is one of only two pieces of pre-18th century gold to be found in Oxford. It went to the college upon the death of George's wife Gertrude. It is made of 22ct gold and is believed to be the work of *Richard Blackwell I*. It is hallmarked London 1661/62 together with the maker's mark depicting a *'hound sejeant'* - that is, a hound in a sitting position on its haunches with front paws on the ground before. In *'A Life of Joseph Hall'* (Lewis, London 1886) the author quotes W.J. Cripps MA, FSA, at some length regarding this awesome cup. Cripps' description, (followed by Lewis who doubtless had no access to the cup for scrutiny) stated: "Hall's cup, cup of gold, circa 1660-70, at Exeter College, Oxford. Cup and cover. It is double-handled, pine-shaped, and repoussé [hammered and shaped from the reverse] with lozenge-shaped gadroons, [convex fluted ruffle-like ornamentation] the upper row of spaces, and the cover ornamented with flowers. Height 6in; width 5in; including handles 6.25in. On the cover are the words Col. Exon. Oxon; and on the cup itself, Col. Exon. Oxon. D.D. Rob. Hall, Ep. Cest. At the bottom 22 carats." Somewhat perplexed by the reference to 'Rob. Hall' vice George, (which I'd seen quoted elsewhere too) I sought guidance from Exeter College, Oxford where Dr Alison Dight was good enough to examine the cup for me under strong artificial light. This scrutiny was revelatory to all parties for it proved that Cripps had been in error by publishing that a reference to

Robert Hall was engraved on this piece. The inscription most definitely reads: **Col. Exon. Oxon. D.D. Geo. Hall, Ep. Cest.** [Donated to Exeter College Oxford by George Hall, Bishop of Chester.] Hopefully, once and for all, any doubts as to the correct wording on the cup are now settled. It was very pleasing to have the enigmatic reference to the wrong donor resolved, though why Cripps had the names so confused is most baffling.

Illustrations © Exeter College, Oxford.

Prior to his appointment to Chester, George became a *Prebendary Canon* (drawing a stipend as a serving canon) at Exeter Cathedral on 23rd December 1639, 'on mandate of Bishop Hall'. On 28th June 1641 George Hall married Gertrude Ameredith, [Meredith] born ca. 1615, (daughter of Edward Ameredith and Margaret Marler) in Mullion, Cornwall. Their marriage was to have no issue. He later succeeded his brother Robert as Archdeacon of Cornwall 'on mandate of the bishop' and was installed on 8th October 1641. After the Restoration in 1660 he became a Chaplain to King Charles II and a Canon of Windsor, followed by his appointment as Archdeacon of Canterbury that same year. He became Bishop of Chester in 1662 and during his tenure of that office he also used the family Coat of Arms – *Sable, three talbots heads erased Argent langued Gules* – which were awarded to his father, (and heirs) in 1631 whilst his father Joseph Hall was Bishop of Exeter. George espoused his father's moderation in devotional matters and was strongly in favour of conformity within the Anglican liturgy. Concurrent with his duties at Chester, George also served as Rector of All Saint's Parish Church, Wigan. He held both posts until his rather extraordinary death in 1668.

Bishop George Hall had a residence in Wigan where he sometimes stayed. It was whilst simply taking a walk on the terrace in the garden of this house on 23rd August 1668 that he accidentally tripped and fell onto a knife he kept in a pocket -- fatally wounding himself in consequence. According to the records at All Saints Wigan, he was buried in the Sanctuary of the church the very next day.

He has a mural memorial on the south wall in All Saints Parish Church, Wigan. The lettering is in Latin but the following is a fair translation sent to me from the church by Kenneth Talbot:

> *Yonder* [that is, in the Sanctuary where the bishop is buried]
> *awaiting the sounding of the last trumpet, laid in sacred dust the*
> *ashes of him who lest this stone should deceive by a lying epitaph,*
> *bade this only be engraven on the tomb [memorial]*
> *George Hall, professor of Theology, an unprofitable but devoted*
> *servant of God's Church, the son or rather the shade of Dr. Joseph*
> *Hall, most holy Bishop, first of Exeter, then of Norwich, destined*
> *ever to live in his writings. Between six and seven years he filled*
> *unworthily the See of Chester, and left this life in the year of his*
> *age fifty-five, of Christ, 1668.*
> *Marvel, reader, at the Bishop's humility.*
> *Seek the rest elsewhere.*

Is it surprising that there is no mention of his unusual death? Are we to assume that George Hall lingered long enough before his last moments so as to dictate his wishes as regards the precise wording of his memorial? It's hazardous to guess. However, one phrase that lingers on reading the epitaph is the mirthful pun on 'son' and implied 'sun' [shade]. Surely more than a clue that George not only had his father's wit but some influence on the text of his memorial too? It's not difficult to empathise with George Hall who obviously seems to be implying that his father's bright and illustrious career could only ever cast a shadow over his children.

Here's another perplexing observation about George Hall. We have already noted his sad accidental demise on 23rd September 1668. However, when his widow Gertrude came to prove his will at Canterbury in December that same year, it was found, (rather astonishingly) to have been drawn up on *22nd of September* – the very day before his tragic death! How extraordinary. One is compelled to think this must have been either a rather amazingly fortuitous coincidence or as the result of some strange episode of precognition. With the Halls you can never quite rule out the fanciful.

George Hall had at least two books published. *'God's Appearing for the Tribe of Levi', (1665)* and a satirical work, *'The Triumphs of Rome over Despised Protestancie', (1655).*

In his will George rather unexpectedly left all his wealth and estate, (at Trentham St. Germans) to Exeter College, Oxford. This may have sparked some family friction – see the entry for Samuel Hall below, George also left provision for his wife Gertrude during her lifetime, (which actually only lasted some seven months after his own death) and a gift of £100 to the poor in his town of birth, (Waltham Abbey). The beautiful gold cup and cover, previously mentioned above, were donated to Exeter College on the death of his wife on 16th March 1669.

Samuel Hall
(1616-1674)

The fourth son Samuel, (probably named after a paternal uncle of that name) was appointed a Prebendary at Exeter Cathedral towards the end of 1640 and installed there as a Canon on 4th February 1641, and within months was appointed as Sub-Dean on 23rd September 1641 – both positions being filled 'on mandate of the bishop' - his father! He was married and had two daughters, Elizabeth, no doubt named after her grandmother, and Mary. Both received sums of money, (£300 and £100 respectively) in their grandfather's will – *see Chapter Five.*

Elizabeth was to go on and marry her cousin Bamfilde Rodd. Mary married Sir Thomas Walker of Exeter ca. 1665. Samuel was appointed sole Executor of his father's estates and inherited land in Totnes, Devon. Samuel contested his older brother George's will when he discovered that, apart from leaving security to his widow, all of his brother's estate was bequeathed to Exeter College, Oxford. Samuel, with two daughters to marry off at some point perhaps was looking for a dowry-funding source. The legal challenge was, I believe, fruitless.

Mary Hall
(1617-1638)

Mary, the second daughter, was born at Waltham. She married James Rodd of Exeter in that cathedral on 29th November 1636. They had one child, a son named Bamfilde. Mary died on Christmas Day 1638 having been married just over two years. She is buried in Exeter Cathedral. Her son Bamfilde married his cousin Elizabeth Hall – the eldest daughter of Samuel Hall, son of Bishop Joseph Hall who left her £300 in his will. This marriage must have been sometime after 21st July 1654 for we know that Elizabeth was classed a minor at that date when bishop Joseph Hall's will was drawn up.

John Hall
(1618?-1650)

The fifth son, John, is likely to have been named after his paternal grand father. The Halls declared that their youngest son was Edward, so it seems reasonable to place John's birth accordingly somewhere logical in the birth date stream. I am minded to place John's birth in ca.1618 for we know it must have been after 1613 and cannot have been as late as 1619, this date being 'reserved' for Edward. Not much is recorded of John's life apart from a reference to him having studied at Oxford, (like his brothers Robert, George and Edward) and we can perhaps also safely assume he was also at Exeter College.

If our knowledge of John's life is sketchy we can certainly be more specific about his death, for Blomefield states that he was laid to rest inside St. Bartholomew's Church, Heigham, Norwich, in 1650. Another reference quotes that John Hall was buried the day he died, according to the burial register of the church. Very significantly, Blomefield gives the following detailed description of the legend carved upon John Hall's grave slab in his 'History of Norfolk' (City of Norwich Chapter 3 Part 1 page 580) published in 1806:

> Hic Johannes Hall. JOSEPHI
> Filius in Legibus Baccalaureus
> Dormivi Suaviter in Domino
> Febr. 12. A° Salut: 1650
> Resurrecturus olim in gloria

A translation of this would be:
> Here lies John Hall. Son of JOSEPH
> Batchelor of Law

Now sweetly sleeping with the Lord
He died February 12th in the year of Salvation: 1650
May he rise one day in glory

Whilst searching through a box of papers relating to bishop Joseph Hall at the Norfolk Record Office, (NRO) I was delighted to find a very interesting letter sent in 1957 to the distinguished Norfolk writer, historian and biographer *Robert Wyndham Ketton-Cremer*, (1906-1969) who, until his death lived at Felbrigg Hall near Cromer, in Norfolk. This letter throws a bit more light onto John Hall, as well as his father. The writer of the letter, J.F. Williams, had obviously been to a recent local history talk given by Ketton-Cremer and this event prompted Williams to inform Ketton-Cremer by letter dated 13th October 1957, that a W.G. Baker MA had travelled from Edinburgh to Norwich some two years previously whilst researching Bishop Hall.

An extract from the letter, [reproduced below - **with my bold lettering**] states that Williams had taken Baker to the St. Bartholomew's Church site on 2nd October 1955 - only two years after the photograph, *(below)* was taken by Norwich photographer George Swain in 1953. **[Image © Norfolk County Council Library and Information Service]** From this picture we can fully appreciate the comment about Bishop Hall's grave being obscured for this is the scene, (or worse) pictured below that confronted Messrs. Williams and Baker when the latter

". . . took several snap-shots of the Bishop's grave in the chancel. The rubbish had been cleared from the slab but the surface was very flaked & I suspect it is still worse now. I enclose two prints which Mr Baker sent me, and a fair amount of the inscription (Bloomefield [sic] iii 580) can be made out. The "Vale Lector"

also occurs on the brass to his son Edward (1642) in the Cathedral. **The adjoining slab at Heigham commemorates another son John, I think.** *I was interested in what you said about the slab* [Joseph's?] *having been moved from the?centre of the chancel in ?1878. It is quite likely that this may have been so in order to fit in with the new paving. Is there any record of this having been done? Many thanks for a most interesting lecture.*
Yrs sincerely
J.F. Williams

Frustratingly there was no letter of reply from Ketton-Cremer in the box file. Much could be said about the contents of the above letter but suffice it to say that John's grave slab had obviously deteriorated substantially between Blomefield's visit in 1806 and that of Messrs Williams and Baker in 1955. Perhaps that is not at all surprising as, if it were indeed positioned in the central chancel area, many feet would have trodden over it between 1806 and 1955 and it would additionally have been subjected to severe heat damage by the devastating incendiary bombs in April1942.

Pleasingly, two of the 'several snaps' taken by Baker and forwarded to Ketton-Cremer by Williams, were in the box file at NRO. Both are monochrome glossy prints. One shows Joseph Hall's grave slab, rather flaked and certainly cracked. At least half of the lettering is missing when compared to the full legend detailed in *Chapter Five*. Again, one is drawn to conclude that the savage heat during the 1942 air-raid quite possibly 'lifted' some of the surface layer of the stone in various segmental areas. The reverse of this print is inscribed *"Heigham Church. Bishop Hall's graveslab. Oct 1955"*

The second photographic print shows bishop Hall's slab, (identifiable) and alongside it another which is very badly cracked, with indistinct features. Williams believed this slab to be John Hall's grave marker. The lack of any discernable lettering is rather unfortunate to say the least. The two grave slabs are not of uniform length either - that for Joseph Hall being at least several, (possibly 6) inches longer than the adjacent slab in question. There is no inscription written on the reverse of this second photo. Sadly, neither of these very interesting photographs are of good enough quality to merit reproduction in this book.

Was Williams actually able to see some detail not picked up by the rather amateurish 'snap' or did he have some other corroborative information linking that slab to John Hall? For instance, did Williams know, (via some other printed reference he did not quote to Ketton-Cremer) that Blomefield had seen this slab in the same position next to Joseph Hall's grave slab back in 1806? Sadly, at this distance in time, with neither Joseph's nor John's grave slabs being extant, (as far as we know) we cannot be more unequivocal about it. However, I am minded to the view that, notwithstanding all the circumstantial evidence of proximity to Joseph Hall's grave slab etc., that Baker did not photograph John Hall's memorial slab in 1955 - for one quite simple reason.

If Williams had been able to access a copy of *Bishop Hall, his life and times* by John Jones, (1826) he would have had at the very least a serious reason to ponder further on the matter of John Hall's grave attribution. On page 421 of this important work, Jones states that John Hall was indeed buried in St. Bartholomew's Church on 12th February 1650 – but that the grave slab was no longer to be found in the church. Jones had been informed that it had been removed some years prior to his 1826 researches, and that it could then be found having a new existence - as the principle stepping-stone built into a stile that allowed for access to the churchyard from its north side!

This outcome, if true, is surely rather inexplicable, for, why would anyone wish to remove a grave slab from the church in order to use it in such a discreditable fashion? I find it even harder to conceive of its use in this way if it was indeed the memorial slab of the fourth son of the famous Joseph Hall, for surely that would have been enough to render it immune to such an ignominious fate? The only credence which can be attached to this story is that one has to assume that the eye-witness-cum-informant, who spoke to John Jones in 1826, was convinced by virtue of readable carved lettering on the stile, that it was indeed a portion of John Hall's grave slab. A very sad and unsatisfactory outcome if true. There's no sign of it on site now.

Edward Hall
(1619-1642)

The sixth and youngest son, Edward, died tragically young aged 23. We do not know his cause of death. There is a reference to him being a scholar at

Exeter College, Oxford prior to his death. We know that his parents were totally grief-stricken at his loss for this fact is mentioned on Edward's extant memorial brass in Norwich Cathedral. Blomefield says that Edward's body was laid to rest by the seventeenth northern pillar, which, counting from the west end of the building precisely coincides with the pillar on which the memorial plate can be found today, adjacent to the high altar. There is far more to be said about Edward's memorial in *Chapter 4.*

Ann Hall
(1622-1660)

Ann, the third daughter, was born at Waltham and may well have been named after her father's first patroness, Lady Ann Drury of Hawstead, Suffolk. Ann married Gascoigne Weld, (1617-1701) of Illington, nr Thetford, Norfolk, in 1640. She died, (named *Anna* on her grave slab) on 19th February 1659/60 aged 55 and is buried in St. Nicholas' Church, Bracon Ash, Norfolk. I believe they had at least three children:

> *Elizabeth*, (Weld) baptised 22nd August 1645 and died 4th December 1714 aged 69. She married Richard Rutter of Kingsley, Cheshire.
> *Mary*, (Weld) baptised 2nd September 1647 as *'Marie'*, who later married the Revd. William Starkey, of Pulham, Norfolk in 1685.
> *Joseph*, (Weld) baptised 29th December 1651 and died unmarried and intestate in London on 18th January 1712. He was elected as MP for Bury St. Edmunds and is buried in the crypt of St. Mary's church by the cathedral. *(See also pages 35 & 36).*

Gascoigne Weld married again, (two years after Ann's death) in 1662 to Philippa Calthorpe (ca. 1629-1701) with whom he had a daughter *Barbara*, (1672-1690). *Philippa* died on 4th August 1701 aged 72 and is buried, with daughter *Barbara* in St. Nicholas' Church, Bracon Ash, Norfolk. Philippa may well have been known as 'Phillip' within her family for she is named thus on her grave slab in St. Nicholas' Church, Bracon Ash. Her husband, Gascoigne Weld died just months before her on 25th April 1701.

His memorial, (also in St. Nicholas' Church Bracon Ash) rather curiously includes a reference to 'infants Judith and Anna.' Should we assume these children were two more daughters he had with his second wife Philippa? Research has so far failed to establish this for certain.

APPENDIX B

A full and new listing of the silverware and one small glass item retrieved from the disastrous fire when St. Bartholomew's was Blitzed on 29th April 1942. Much of this information is hitherto unpublished. *All photographs of silverware by the Author, by very kind permission of Francesca Vanke, Curator of Decorative Art, Norwich Museums Service.*

Items 1 & 2

Chalice – an Elizabethan Communion cup bearing the Norwich Castle and Lion stamp together with the date letter 'C' for 1567 and the maker's mark - a flat fish. See *below* for details of the maker's identity.

Paten Cover – same marks and date. Around the circumference on the 'foot' the following lettering –

SENT ✶ BARTELMEVS ✶ OF ✶ HAYHAM

And running horizontally across the middle the date –1567

[Illustration showing the Chalice of 1567 with its unsightly rim repair patch. Norwich Museums Service Ref No. 1946.28.1]

These items both just pre-date Joseph's birth, (1574) but would almost certainly have been handled by him when administering, or indeed receiving, the sacraments at Holy Communion. Both pieces were made in Norwich at a time when the city's silversmiths would have been very busy completing newly commissioned silverware, following a ruling that all ancient Chalices and Patens were to be replaced by new Cups with Covers. However, there is a view that this cup could have been reworked from an earlier item. Nigel Bumphrey, (Norwich Diocesan Advisor for Silver) is of this view and cites the fact that the silver is so very thin – often a typical sign of remodelling. We examined this item in Norwich Museum on 18th October 2011 and I was shown where the patterning around the cup's circumference had actually split through the metal, almost certainly necessitating repair contemporary with the probable reworking. There is also a rather ugly patch repair to a split in the cup's rim.

Dating this remedial work is nigh on impossible. When the rim of this piece is lightly tapped it has a very 'thin' resonance.

The Paten Cover has a particularly interesting story to reveal, for when the silverware had been removed from the safe in 1942 after the destructive air-raid the previous night, it was only by pure chance that the Paten Cover was found. According to an account I have read in Vol XXVIII Part IV of a *Norfolk Archaeological Society* paper published in 1945, the much-battered safe and its precious contents had been removed from the smouldering church site to the relative nearby sanctuary of 168 Nelson Street, Norwich, the home of a Mrs. Bream. My *Kelly's Directory for Norwich dated 1954* indeed lists a Mrs. Ethel Lucy Bream as a shopkeeper at this address. The Revd. J.F. Williams, Rector of South Walsham Church, Norfolk and a Canon Peck were in attendance at Mrs. Bream's house inspecting the rescued silverware when Canon Peck appears to have decided to have a final check of the damaged safe.

Fortuitously this inspection revealed the presence of the somewhat blackened Paten Cover hiding up one corner. It was sent for expert scrutiny after cleaning, and this is when it gave up its secret, for it was discovered to have originally been a flat circular 'paten', (communion cup cover) which had subsequently been cleverly re-fashioned at a later date, into a lid-type cup cover, with the addition of a circular 'foot' which contained the inscription mentioned above.

[Illustration above showing the inscription SENT ★ BARTELMEVS ★ OF ★ HAYHAM on the 'foot' of the Paten Cover of 1567. Norwich Museums Service Ref. No. 1945.54]

The re-modelling work had obviously been given to a Norwich silversmith who had added the contemporary Norwich mark – castle & lion: his own mark, (a flat fish); and the date letter 'C' assigned to the year 1567. At the time of its scrutiny and subsequent repair in ca.1942 the 'flat fish' mark was not generally ascribed with any accuracy to a definable maker. However, Nigel Bumphrey informs me that the unusual mark is now positively identified as that belonging to **Thomas Buttell** – whose surname corresponds in its first syllable, (Butt) to a Norfolk word for a flounder – a 'flat fish'. We also examined this piece on 18th October 2011.

Items 3 & 4

Chalice and Paten – Very large, and marked with a Lion's head, (erased) plus Britannia. Date stamped 'm' in a calligraphic style, (London 1707) and bearing the maker's initials 'SL' for **Gabriel Sleath.** Chalice inscribed around its middle circumference: 'Ecclesiae Sti Bartholomei de hegham juxta Norvic. Sacrum, JWRr, 1707.'
[*The church of Saint Bartholomew Heigham near Norwich. Sacred. JWRr, 1707.*]
In my judgement the initials in this inscription may be accurately assigned to
J(ohn) **W**(hitefoot -) **R**(ecto)**r** 1707.

When the rim of this piece is lightly tapped it has a mellow, bell-like resonant 'ring'. It is undoubtedly a wonderful item.
[Illustration above showing the Chalice of 1707. Norwich Museums Service Ref. No. 1946.28.2]

Confusingly, there were two Rectors of this church named John Whitefoot – father and son – and the elder one conducted Joseph Hall's memorial service at St. Peter Mancroft Church, Norwich, on 30th September 1656. I'm positive that the enigmatic initials described above belong to the son, John Whitefoot jnr, Rector from 1682-1731. Upon very close inspection of the

119

chalice, the paten cover and its knob, Nigel Bumphrey noticed separate assay markings on all three components, concluding that the knob of the paten cover had been assayed separately prior to being attached to the paten. This was very interesting information and unlikely to have been previously noted.

[Illustration above showing the 1707 Paten Cover by Gabriel Sleath. Norwich Museums Service Ref. No. 1946.28.2.1]

Item 5

Paten – Inscribed on base:
Heigham 1656
This piece has abnormal stamp marks consisting of:
A rose without a stem
A crown as used in Norwich ca. 1650
Maker's mark of A R?
Crossed, net-like, lines. [Unique to this item?]

[Illustrations showing the1656 Arthur Haslewood II Paten plus 'foot' (left) and a close up of the beautiful engraving within the 'foot' (right). Norwich Museums Service Ref. No. 1946.28.3]

Nigel Bumphrey had suggested to me that another silverware specialist, the late Geoffrey Barrett, had been minded to re-interpret the maker's mark 'A R' [noted by The Rev E.C. Hopper in Norfolk Archaeology Vol XVI page 246 (pub. 1907] as **'A H'** which, if now corroborated by Nigel on our viewing of this piece on 18th October 2011, would transport it into another realm of significance, for this would assign it to the redoubtable Haslewood dynasty of Norwich silversmiths. Happily Nigel was able to positively confirm that there was enough evidence in the second letter to declare it to be a letter **'H'** and that he was minded therefore to judge it a piece by **Arthur Haslewood II**, (1638-84). It was a joyous moment.

I had long been intrigued by the lettering 'Heigham 1656' on its base, for this was the very year of Bishop Joseph Hall's death. Although the piece does not bear any memorial inscription can we believe its making in that significant year was pure coincidence? Bearing in mind that Parliament had declared him a 'delinquent' in 1643 and then ousted him from office and his original palace at the cathedral, perhaps it was not considered wise or appropriate to name him on the object. Certainly an enigma.

Item 6
Chalice – London date stamp for 1871. Maker's initials H L H L for **Henry Lias & Sons**, plus other marks for the year. Also inscribed:
In loving Memory of Eliza Browne Fitch, Woodlands, Heigham, obiit August 10th, 1885. I will receive the Cup of Salvation and will call upon the name of the Lord.

Unhappily it must be declared that the current whereabouts of this Chalice is unknown. It seems to have disappeared from the silver record. One must hope that further research will bring forth information leading to its discovery. I think there is a significant worry that it may well have been unofficially 'gifted' elsewhere at some point. It is most irregular for this to have happened and of course it also means that there is no official record of where it went or when. All very unsatisfactory one has to say. Investigations are continuing of course.

Item 7
Flagon – Glass with silver mounts. Date stamped 'C' for London 1878, maker's initials T P plus other marks for that year. The mount was inscribed:
Presented to S. Bartholomew's Church, Heigham, by E.M. Goulburn, Dean of Norwich, in memory of Bishop Hall, Dec 10, 1878.

This 19th century item can certainly be retrospectively linked to Bishop Joseph Hall if only for its memorial inscription. The Right Reverend Edward Meyrick Goulburn, (1818-1897) was Dean of Norwich 1866-1889.

Although the gift is seemingly in the Dean's name perhaps we can assume that, in reality, it was a gift of benevolent support and encouragement from the whole Norwich Diocese, in recognition of the significant building work witnessed in the completion of a new north aisle extension to St. Bartholomew's church as already covered elsewhere.

Illustration showing a glass flagon with silver mounts. Re-drawn by the Author from an indistinct original taken from an anonymous catalogue of this period. It is very likely that the Dean Goulbourn gift was very similar to this. Original image from Nigel Bumphrey's collection.

Very sadly, we currently have no idea what happened to this most interesting flagon when St Bartholomew's Church was Blitzed on the night of 29th April 1942. I think one can assume that its memorial status together with its valuable three-part silver mount set, would have normally assured its protection in the safe when not in use. When the safe was blown out of the vestry wall we might easily consider the glass surely shattered - but what of the silver mounts? In discussion with Nigel Bumphrey I came to the conclusion that the description of the piece, *(above, at the head of this listing)* was scantly wanting, for this item would have been potentially far more significant in reality. The maker's initials **'T P'**, (not identified in 1907) actually belonged to **Thomas Peard**, a well-known specialist silver plate worker established in London.

It should be explained that the three silver items were (i) a heavy circular 'foot', (ii) a top handle-come-spout construction made to fit onto the 'shoulders' of the glass globe, and (iii) a narrow thin band with decorative lettering, which had a fitment allowing it to (a) be attached to the handle component and (b) to allow the silver band to hug the central circumference of the glass globe under tension from the handle fitment - *see line illustration above*. A scale indicator on the indistinct catalogue picture suggested that the flagon would have been some sixteen inches in height when fully assembled. Rather amazingly Nigel Bumphrey actually had access to a very similar set of three silver components from yet another flagon set also made by **Thomas Peard**, this time date-lettered for 1877 – only one year before he made the now missing flagon set, gifted to St.

Bartholomew's Church by Dean Goulburn in 1878. Surely the missing flagon components of 1878 *must* have had very similar silver components in its fittings?

Thomas Peard, who specialised in this type of work, had doubtless made any number of these silver memorial flagon units. What a great sadness it is that we do not know the whereabouts of that very special 1878 silver mount set with its precious dedication memorial inscription to bishop Joseph Hall.

Item 8

Quite amazingly, one delightfully frail item of glassware somehow managed to avoid destruction that night in April 1942. The precise function this exquisite blue glass jug or ewer had at St. Bartholomew's is not known. It measures just seven inches in height and bears lovely floral patterning. A note in the Norfolk Records Office says that *'a lady'* rescued it from the blitzed church ruins and that she gave it to the Saint Barnabas Counselling Centre many years later *'in gratitude.'* Mr Terence Burkill, who for many years served as Churchwarden at St. Barnabas' Church, Norwich, recalls having heard that the donor lived in the Nelson Street area

 at the time of its discovery. Could this lady have been Mrs. Ethel Lucy Bream of 168 Nelson Street, who we mentioned earlier? Another possibility is that the lady concerned was Miss Elsie Haverson, (who I personally knew very well during my 21 years as organist at St. Barnabas' Church) who for many years was a Churchwarden at St. Bartholomew's and who had a close personal link with the work of The St. Barnabas Counselling Centre. Whoever the donor was we must be grateful that such a fragile item has survived. It is now cared for at St. Barnabas' Parish Church, Norwich. From close inspection I would date the object to ca. 1870-1900.

[Photographed by the Author, courtesy of the Parochial Church Council St. Barnabas Parish Church, Norwich]

APPENDIX C

Official correspondence concerning the exhumation and reburial of Bishop Joseph Hall as held by Norfolk Records Office. (Diocesan Faculty 0084/74).

Letter from Rt. Revd. Maurice Wood, Bishop of Norwich, to Oliver Prior, Diocesan Registrar, dated 27/06/1974.

Dear Oliver,

I am concerned about the present situation of Bishop Hall's grave. It is in the bombed ruins of St Bartholomew's Church, covered by a stone now very worn, where the Chancel once stood. As you will know, it is planned to transfer the churchyard of St Bartholomew's to the City for an open space.

It is, this year, the 400th anniversary of Bishop Hall's birth, and I wonder w[h]ether it could be possible to arrange for his remains to be buried, perhaps in the Cathedral or its precincts, if the Dean & Chapter were agreeable. I would like your opinion, therefore, on a number of questions.

    a) Do you think it is a possibility that such a re-burial can be arranged,
        assuming the support of the Dean & Chapter?

    b) How soon do you think it might take place, because it would be better to do it in this centenary year, if possible?

    c) Would there be, do you think, any objections to having the remains cremated before reburial if the Dean & Chapter wanted this?

    d) Would we need any search to be made for surviving relatives, even after 320 years, or would we need to look for consent in any way?

    e) In the light of negotiations at present with the city, would their consent also be needed?

    f) Are there any further implications to this possibility, that occur to you which I have not covered?

I would be most grateful for your help with this matter. I have written to the Dean, also, asking for his tentative reactions at this stage.

Yours ever,

Maurice.

Note from Oliver Prior in answer to the Bishop's questions, dated 3/7/74
    a) Yes, if Chancellor grants a Faculty for exhumation.
    b) This is for the Chapter, but there would be no reason for delay.
    c) This would be a matter for the Chapter.
    d) No
    e) No
    f) Not that I am aware of.
    Yours sincerely,
    [file copy not signed]

*Letter from the Archdeacon, Timothy Dudley-Smith, to Oliver Prior,
dated 27/09/74*

Dear Oliver,
BISHOP HALL'S GRAVE
As I think you, and others, know from his recent letters, the Bishop
would like to see Bishop Hall's remains removed from the old
churchyard of St Bartholomew's which is to become a playground,
(I understand); and transferred to the Cathedral. And feels that this
centenary year of Bishop Hall's Birth, (death?) would be a very
appropriate time.

The Cathedral have now agreed that they would be happy to have a
simple Service at which his ashes (assuming that what remains of
his bones can be cremated after exhumation) would be scattered in
the cloisters, and a small memorial tablet erected.

This being so, we ought to proceed without delay if we are to get it
done this year. Can you very kindly tell me what is the next step?
Is this in fact something you should undertake for the Bishop; or
something I should try to do for him?

I imagine we need to make a Faculty application for this
exhumation (and cremation?); and I would be glad if, supposing
you think I should act in this, you would let me have a form of
application with direction about who would be the proper person(s)
to make the application. I think there is no longer an incumbent of
St Bartholomew's, nor PCC, nor church wardens, as it is on the

way to being merged with St Barnabas Heigham, but the process, I think, is not complete!

Do we require any Civic authority? Or to notify the Superintendent Registrar of an exhumation and reburial. I am afraid all this is very foreign ground to me; and if you felt you should handle it I should of course be delighted!

Yours sincerely,
Timothy

Note from Oliver Prior to the Archdeacon dated 16/10/74

Dear Timothy,

Bishop Hall Grave

Thankyou for your letter of 27 September which I regret I have not acknowledged before now.

A Faculty is required for the exhumation of human remains and in view of the somewhat unusual nature of this case I will seek the Chancellor's views and his directions as to the appropriate party to make the application.

[file copy not signed]

Handwritten note [19/10/74]

Registrar

Bishop Hall's remains

There ought to be no difficulty here. But how does it arise? Is this churchyard becoming a play park under the open spaces Act, as if so I will deal with the matter on the local authority's petition. Otherwise the Archdeacon ought to [make?] a Petition supported by a letter of request from the Bishop and a letter of proposal for the re-interment signed by the Dean & Chapter (or their clerk). I am not in favour of ancient remains being cremated: it has its objections. The proper course is for such remains as may exist to be put in a small casket and re-interred.

[signed] JWM 19/10/74

Short note from Oliver Prior to the Archdeacon, dated 23/10/1974

Dear Timothy

Bishop Hall's Grave

Further to my note of 16th Oct I now enclose a copy of the
Chancellor's observations on this matter which I hope will be of
assistance.

Yours sincerely

[file copy not signed]

***Letter from Colin Pordham, (Chapter Clerk) to the Worshipful
Chancellor of the Diocese of Norwich. Faculty Petition – St
Bartholomew's Churchyard Norwich, dated 3rd December 1974.***
Bishop Hall's Grave.

On behalf of the Dean & Chapter I confirm that the Chapter have
agreed that a small casket containing the remains of Bishop Hall
may be intered in the Cloister Garth of the Cathedral Church of
Norwich, the reburial to be marked by an appropriate service and
commemorative tablet.

Yours faithfully

C. Pordham

Chapter Clerk

***Letter from Colin Pordham, (Chapter Clerk), to Oliver Prior, Diocesan
Registrar, dated 3rd December 1974.***

Dear Mr Prior

Bishop Hall

The Chapter have agreed to the re-interment in the Cloister Garth
of the remains of Bishop Hall and at the request of the Archdeacon
I enclose his Petition with the supporting letter from the Bishop
and a formal letter of consent to the reinterment by the Dean &
Chapter. I would be grateful if you could let me know as soon as a
date for the reburial service has been fixed.

Yours sincerely

Colin Pordham

Chapter Clerk

***Letter from Oliver Prior to C. Pordham dated 6th December 1974
Faculty Petition – St Bartholomew's Churchyard Norwich. Bishop Hall's
Grave.***

Thankyou for your letter of 3rd December with the enclosed letter
of consent and the accompanying petition from the Archdeacon of

Norwich. I will now pass this application to the Chancellor for his directions and I will let you hear further as soon as possible.

Yours sincerely

[file copy not signed]

Letter from Oliver Prior to the Archdeacon dated 13th December 1974

My dear Archdeacon

Faculty Petition – St Bartholomew's, Heigham

Your application for a faculty to exhume the remains of Bishop Hall has been completed by the Chancellor who has made the following Order:

1) Dispense with Citation
2) Faculty to issue
3) Liberty to apply if necessary as to arrangements should any query or difficulty arise.

Accordingly I now enclose the Faculty Deed herewith.

The Chapter Clerk, Mr Colin Pordham, has requested that he should be informed as soon as a date for the reburial has been arranged. I have sent Mr Pordham a copy of this letter and should be grateful if you could kindly contact him.

[file copy copy not signed]

Letter from Peter Taylor Funeral Services Ltd, Norwich, to Oliver Prior, (Coroner) dated 21st January 1975

Dear Sir

St Bartholomew's Heigham

Exhumation of Joseph Hall

We wish to inform you that we hold a Faculty for the Exhumation of Bishop Joseph Hall from the churchyard of the Old Church for the reburial in the cloister garth of the Cathedral Church of Norwich.

We shall inform you of the day and time in due course, in case you wish your official to be present, if not we will advise you what we find when the grave is opened.

Yours faithfully

Peter Taylor

Letter from the Archdeacon, Timothy Dudley-Smith, to Oliver Prior, Diocesan Registrar, dated 22/05/75

128

My Dear Oliver,

The Faculty that you sent me authorising the exhumation and re-burial of the remains of Bishop Hall states on it that I should certify to you when the work authorised has been completed. In fact, his remains in a small casket were buried yesterday in the Cloister garth, at a delightful Service conducted by the Vice Dean, at which the Bishop was present and gave a short Address. It was a most seemly occasion, and I think those present felt it fitting that Bishop Hall, having been excluded from his rights in his lifetime, should now have his earthly remains resting in his own cathedral.

May I certify by this letter that, the action authorised by the Chancellor's Faculty have been completed?

Yours
Timothy.

The Faculty Petition Document

The Faculty Petition itself is a four-page *pro-forma* document with many clauses and questions, most of which did not apply to this rather extraordinary, not to say unique, circumstance. It was filled in by hand in blue/black ink by the Archdeacon, The Ven. Timothy Dudley-Smith. We may ignore the majority of this document but there are two entries that must be noted. On page two is a 'Description of Works' with a sub-heading 'Schedule' and here the Archdeacon sets out what needs doing:

1) The exhumation of the remains of Bishop Hall from St Bartholomew's Churchyard.
2) For the purpose of this re-burial, with an appropriate Service and commemorative tablet, in the Cloister Garth of the Cathedral at Norwich.

Another comment by the Petitioner declares that it will be necessary to 'interfere' with an existing already 'badly cracked, defaced, and barely decipherable stone'.

The Faculty Petition, which had been sent to Oliver Prior, (the Diocesan Registrar) for authorisation on behalf of the Dean & Chapter by its Clerk, Colin Pordham, on 3rd December 1974 - was granted on 13th December 1974.

Bishop Maurice Wood's hope for a re-interment of Joseph Hall's remains in 1974, (the 400th anniversary year of his birth in 1574) must have looked impossible by early December 1974. Doubtless the paperwork involved with the Faculty Petition had eaten up many more weeks than perhaps originally envisaged. It was a nice idea though. However, we now know it was not possible to go ahead with the re-interment until some five months later on 21st May 1975.

Filed within the Faculty papers, in addition to all the letters and notes already described above, it was very moving indeed to find that someone had most thoughtfully appended a copy of the Order of Service for the re-burial. The inclusion of this document seemed to not only appropriately close bishop Maurice Wood's enterprising mission, but also to fittingly end my own personal quest on behalf of the worthy bishop Joseph Hall of Norwich.

Norwich Cathedral
INTERMENT OF ASHES OF JOSEPH HALL
BISHOP OF NORWICH 1641-56
MAY 21, 1975

SENTENCES said by Canon Frank Colquhoun Vice Dean

PSALM 23 sung by members of Cathedral Choir

LESSON read by the Ven. T. Dudley-Smith Archdeacon of Norwich

ADDRESS by the Rt Rev the Bishop of Norwich

BURIAL OF ASHES

PRAYERS said by the Vice Dean

MOTET 'God be in my head' sung by the Choristers

BLESSING by the Bishop

INDEX

A

á Kempis, Thomas – influence on Joseph Hall **22**

All Saint's Parish Church, Hawstead, Suffolk –
　　　　　　Joseph's appointment to **15**

All Saint's Parish Church, Wigan, Lancashire –
　　　　　　connection with George Hall **109**

Aylward, Richard – *organist/composer* at Norwich Cathedral at
　　　　　　'Restoration' in 1660 **79**

Arminius, Jacobus – founder of *Arminianism*. (See also *Dort Synod*) **29**

Ashmolean Museum, The – Oxford University **109**

B

Bacon, Sir Edmund – *brother* of Lady Ann Drury of Hawstead **21**

Baldwin, William – *vice Prefect* English Mission in Brussels -
　　　　　　Joseph's encounter with **21**

Bancanquall, Dr Walter – delegate to *Dort Synod* **28**

Beating the Bounds – restored to correct observance season **48**

Biljaar, Willem van – struck Dort medals **32-34**

Blomefield, Francis – historian **49, 112, 114-115**

Blundell's School, Tiverton, Devon – *Joseph declined Master's post* **15**

Bradshaw, William – Joseph's tutor at Ashby Grammar School **2, 5, 8**

Bream, Mrs. Ethel Lucy – parishioner at St. Bartholomew's Parish
　　　　　　Church, Norwich **83, 118, 123**

Brinsley, John – *Headmaster* at Ashby Grammar School **2**

Brent, Sir Nathaniel – Archbishop Laud's *Inquisitor* **49-50, 52**

Browne, Richard – first owner in 1587 of Joseph's *Heigham Palace*
　　　　　　(see also *'Dolphin Inn'*) **76-77**

Browne, Robert (1550-1633) – founder of 'Brownist' radical movement **26**

Browne, Dr (Sir) Thomas – Joseph's physician and friend **69, 71, 84, 90-91**

Buttell, Thomas – Elizabethan silversmith **119**

C

Calthorpe, *Philippa* – married Gascoigne Weld 1662 **116**

Carleton, Dudley – *Ambassador*, The Hague – Joseph's encounter with after
　　　　　　illness at *Dort Synod* **31**

Carleton, Bishop George of Llandaff **28, 31**

Cartwright, Thomas – radical Puritan preacher **26**

Chad(d)erton, Lawrence – Joseph's Master at Emmanuel College **8, 37**

Charles I – Monarch – (1625-49) **38, 40, 45, 47, 56, 62, 105**

Charles II – Monarch at *Restoration* in 1660 (until 1685) **94, 104, 109**

Chester Cathedral – connection with George Hall **108-110**

Cholmley, Hugh – lifelong friend and supporter of Joseph **5, 15, 39**

Christchurch Mansion, Suffolk – location of Lady Drury's *Panels* **23**

Colchester, Essex – where Joseph was Ordained in 1600. **15**

Cook, Mr – generous supporter of Joseph in hardship **64-65**

Corbett, Miles – MP for Great Yarmouth **66**

Corbett, Richard – bishop of Norwich. (1632-35) **48-51**

Costerus, *Father* – Joseph's encounter with **21**

Cromwell, Oliver – Lord Protector during Commonwealth (1649-58) **72, 105**

D

Davenant, John – Prof of Divinity at Cambridge **28**

Dean and Chapter – Norwich Cathedral **58, 79**

Dean and Chapter – Exeter Cathedral **104-105**

Denny, Lord – 1st Earl of Norwich - Joseph's Patron at *Waltham* **25-26**

Dolphin Inn, The – formerly Bishop Hall's Palace ca. 1646-56 **75-76, 78**

Doncaster, *Viscount* – re Mission to France with Joseph 1616 **27, 34**

Donne, John – poet and Dean St. Paul's Cathedral, London -
> (see also *Dort Medal*) **18-19, 34**

Dort Medal – commemorative piece issued re *Dort Synod* 1618/19 – Joseph
> is awarded rare gold version **32, 34-36, 40**

Dort, Synod of – held in Dordtretch, Holland, to investigate and adjudicate
> on legality of *Arminianism* **28, 31-32, 34**

Drury, Lady Ann – Joseph's Patroness at Hawstead – (see also *Panels*) **15, 23, 116**

Drury, Elizabeth – died 1610 aged 14yrs – Joseph's *Memorial verse* to **18**

Drury, Sir Robert – Joseph's Patron at Hawstead – conflicts with **15-17, 19, 24**

Dudley-Smith, The Ven. Timothy – Archdeacon of Norwich **98, 129-130**

E

Emmanuel College, Cambridge – Joseph's college **4-8, 16, 22, 35-37 39-40, 104**

Exeter College, Oxford – Joseph's sons educated at **104, 107-112, 115**

Exeter – Joseph's1st Bishopric **25, 36-39, 42, 45-46, 48, 87, 90, 104-106, 111**

F

Fitzwilliam Museum, The - Cambridge – custodians of Joseph's
> Gold Dort medal **32-33, 35-36**

G

Gibbs, Richard – organist Norwich Cathedral – made redundant (1643) **79**

Gilby, Revd Anthony –superintendent Ashby Grammar School **2, 4**

Gilby, Nathaniel – son of above and Joseph's tutor at Emmanuel College **4, 7-8**

Gloucester – Bishopric refused by Joseph (1624) **27, 37, 47**

Goad, Dr Thomas – Joseph's replacement at *Dort Synod*. (1619) **28**

Goodwin, Mrs. – staunch supporter of Joseph at imposition
> of *sequestration* (1643) **63, 65, 88-89**

Gostlin, (William?) – staunch supporter of Joseph at *Sequestration* **69, 76**

Goulburn, Rt Revd Edward Meyrick – Dean of Norwich (1866-89) **121-123**

Grandridge, Mr, Revd Minister – *arranged* Joseph's betrothal to *Elizabeth* **20**

Greenwood, John Sheriff of Norwich **– 63, 68, 70**

Green Yard, The – open-air public meeting area in precinct of
           Norwich Cathedral where Joseph preached **70, 72-73**

H

Hall, Joseph & Elizabeth's *Children* – **see *Appendix B***

Hall, Elizabeth – wife (neé Bambridge) **20, 59, 60, 63, 65, 75, 77, 79-80**

Hall, John – Joseph's father. Died 1608 **1, 3-5, 7**

Hall, Joseph, *Bishop* and first English Satirist?

    Meditations, his iconic works **13, 20-25**

    First *poem* published **8**

    First *book* published **9**

    Ordained (1600) **15**

    Appointed Rector at *Hawstead,* Suffolk (1601) **15-20, 24-25, 34, 59**

    Preaches at *Richmond Palace* (1606) **24**

    Personal *chaplain* to Prince Henry **24**

    Appointed *Rector of Waltham Abbey* **25-26, 31-32**

    Defends the Church of England against the *Brownists* **26**

    Appointed *Doctor of Divinity* (1612) **27**

    Preaches *flattering sermon before King James I* (1613) **27**

    Mission to *France* 1616 and illness **27**

    Appointed *Dean of Worcester* 2**7**

    Mission to *Scotland* with King James I in 1617 to impose the
            Five Articles of Perth **27**

    English delegation member to the *Synod of Dort* (1618/19)
            and is awarded prestigious gold medal **28-32**

    Refuses offer of appointment to *Gloucester* (1624) **37**

            Accepts *Exeter* (1627) **38**

    Marries *Elizabeth Winniff* (1603) **20**

    Award of *Arms* 1631 **39**

    A pronouncement on *Graves* inside
            church buildings. (1637) **42**

    Appointed *Bishop of Norwich* (1641) **48**

    Detained in the *Tower of London* (1641/42) **56**

    Pronounced a *Delinquent and Malignant* by Parliament. (1643) -
            degrading sequestration imposed without mercy **62**

    'Hard Measure' written at Heigham. (May1647) **69-70**

    Sequestration eased (1648) **78-79**

    Last surviving sermon preached at St Bartholomew, Heigham on
            1st July 1655 - his 80th birthday **83-84**

    His *death* – the final precious moments recorded by his close
            friend Revd John Whitefoot **85-86, 90**

    His *will* **87-89**

    His *Monument* in St Bartholomew's Church, Heigham **91-93**

His *exhumation and reburial* (1975) **97-102**

Hall, Winifride – Joseph's mother **1-3**

Harrison, Robert – Radical from Norwich **26**

Haslewood II, Arthur - Norwich *silversmith* during Elizabethan era **120-121**

Hastings, Henry – third Earl of Huntingdon **1**

Haverson, Elsie – possible connection with artefact St. Bartholomew's Church Heigham, Norwich **123**

Hawstead, Suffolk – Joseph appointed Rector (1601) **15**

Heigham, Hamlet of – Joseph's 'retirement' Palace-in-exile situated there north of Norwich **75**

Heinsius, Daniel - designer of the Dort Medal **32**

Henry Prince of Wales – son of James I **24**

Hoggett, Richard – Norfolk and Norwich Archaeology Society **83**

Howell, Revd Hinds – Rector of Drayton, Norwich, and *donor of altar dedicated to Bishop Joseph Hall* (1878) **82**

Huntingdon, Earl of – employer of *John Hall*, Joseph's father **1**

J

James I Monarch (1603-1625) – Joseph's service to **19, 27, 30 32, 34, 37, 40**

Jermy, John – married Joseph's granddaughter *Mary Starkey* **35**

Jermy, William – donor of Dort medal to Emmanuel College **35**

Jones, John – biographer of Joseph Hall (1826)   **92,115**

Jonson, Ben – (1572-1637) writer and dramatist **10**

K

Ketton-Cremer, Robert Wyndham – Norfolk historian and biographer **113-115**

L

Laud, William – *Archbishop of* Canterbury **27, 38-39, 43, 47-54, 57**

Leveson, Sir Walter – successfully prosecuted by Joseph for *misappropriating Church revenues in Wolverhampton* **37**

Lias, Henry & Sons – Victorian silversmiths **121**

Lilley, (aka Lyly) William – *odious influence on Joseph at Hawstead* **17-19**

Linton, Revd S – *Rector* of St Bartholomew, Heigham in 1878 **81**

Losinga, Herbert de – first Bishop of Norwich, his tomb in Norwich Cathedral *wrecked by Puritans.* (1643) **94**

M

Marlowe, John (aka *'Christopher'*) (1564-93) – poet, writer, controversialist **12**

Marston, John – (1576-1634) writer, satirist and controversialist – *spats with Joseph* **10, 12**

Meditations – Joseph's *iconic and ground-breaking* works **13, 20-25**

Mildmay, Sir Walter – founder of *Emmanuel College, Cambridge* (1584) **7, 104**

Montague, Richard – Bishop of Norwich (1638-41) **48, 53-56, 59**

N

Nero, Emperor – orders *Seneca* to commit suicide –
(see also *Sene*ca) **9**
Nashe, Thomas (1567-1601) – writer, satirist and controversialist **12**

O

Oldenbarnveldt, Johan van – proponent of *Arminianism* in Netherlands
and controversially beheaded. (1619) **31**

P

Panels – Lady Drury's *Devotional plaques* **23**
Peard, Thomas – Victorian silversmith **122-123**
Pelset, William – *Rector* of Market Bosworth – proposal he be Joseph's
tutor rejected **3, 4**
Peterson, Dr William – *Dean of Exeter* and Joseph's son-in-law **38, 88-89, 107**
Pordham, Colin – *Clerk* to Dean and Chapter, Norwich Cathedral **127-128, 130**
Potts, Sir John of Mannington – Sequestration Appeals member
for Norfolk – Joseph's appeal to **65**
Priesthood – Joseph's entry to (December 1600) **15**
Prior, Oliver – Norwich Diocesan *Registrar* **124-129**
Private Eye – satirical magazine **11**

R

Rawley, John – Sheriff of Norwich – Joseph's encounters with **63**
Remomstrants – followers of *Jacobus Arminius* in Netherlands **29, 31, 45**

S

St Bartholomew's Church, Heigham, Norwich – Joseph's service there as
Assistant priest after his eviction from Norwich Cathedral
79, 85, 97, 122, 124, 127
St Peter Mancroft Church, Norwich – congregational unrest there at
treatment of their priest **54, 86**
St Nicholas' Parish Church, Bracon Ash, Norfolk – Hall family
burials there **116**
Seneca (4BC-65AD) influence of his writings on Joseph's
early works **9**
Sleath, Gabriel – 17th/18th century silversmith **119-120**
Sleigh, Edmund – Joseph's uncle and benefactor **6**
Smith, Harold – former Sacrist at Norwich Cathedral – his special
involvement at *Joseph's reburial* (1975) **99, 101**
Sotherton, Thomas – sequestrator - Joseph's encounter with **63**
Spa, Belgium – Joseph's inclusion in Embassy to, and his controversial
behaviour there **21**
Spenser, Edmund – (1552-99) poet Joseph considered had no equals **13**
Stafford, Sir Edward – English Ambassador to France and Joseph's
contact with **18**

Stapledon, Walter de – founder of *Exeter College, Oxford* (1314) **104**

Starkey, William – Joseph's son-in-law (married Mary Hall) **35, 116**

Stationer's Company, The – their controls on printing and
        publishing in Joseph's lifetime **9-10, 12**

Swift, Jonathan – 18th century writer possibly influenced by one of
        Joseph's books when creating *'Gulliver's Travels'* **22**

T

Taylor, Peter – funeral services, Norwich **128**

Tooley, John – Alderman of Norwich – Joseph's encounter with **63**

V

Virgidemiarum – Joseph's first publication, (a set of six books)
        in his own right **9**

W

Waltham (Abbey) Essex – Joseph's appointment there **25-26, 31-32**

Ward, Dr Samuel – Master, Sydney Sussex College Cambridge **28**

Weld, Gascoigne – Joseph's son-in-law, *(married Ann(a) Hall)* **88-89, 116**

Weld, Joseph – Joseph's *grandson* and MP for Bury St Edmunds **35, 89**

Whitaker, William – Joseph's first published work, (an *'Elegy'*)
        written in memory of **8**

Whitefoot, Revd John – *Priest of St. Bartholomew's Church*, Heigham, Norwich,
        whilst *Joseph served as his assistant* after eviction
        from Norwich Cathedral **80, 86, 90-91, 119**

Whitgift, Dr John – (1530-1604) *Archbishop of Canterbury* **12**

Williams, Revd J.F. – Rector, South Walsham Church, Norfolk **113-118**

Williams, Dr John – *Bishop of London* **47, 57**

Winniff, (aka Whinniff) Elizabeth – Joseph's wife **20**

Winniff, (aka Whinniff) George – Joseph's father-in-law **20**

Wodehouse, Sir Thomas of Kimberley, Norfolk – *Joseph's*
        encounter with **65**

Wood, The Rt Revd Maurice – *Bishop of Norwich* and prime mover
        in Joseph's *reburial in Norwich Cathedral*
        cloister. (1975) **98-102**

Wren, Matthew – bishop of Norwich (1635-38) **48, 51-55, 57, 61**

Reference Bibliography

Akehurst, James
A new History of the Parish of Heigham 2003

Atherton, Ian, with Eric Fernie, Christopher Harper-Bill & Hassell Smith
Norwich Cathedral
Hambleton Press 1996

Delves, E.
A Brief History of the Hamlet of Heigham, Norwich
Norfolk News 1879

Gittings, Clare
Death, burial and the individual in Early Modern England
Routledge: New York 1988

Hall, Joseph
Observations of some Specialities of Divine Providence in the Life of Joseph Hall
1647
This autobiography, and other of his works, are freely available and readable as a digitised facsimile edition. They may be found on several website sources.

Jones, Revd. John
Bishop Hall, his life and times
L.B. Seeley & Sons, London 1826

Ketton-Cremer, R.W.
Norfolk in the Civil War
Archon 1977

Ketton-Cremer, R.W.
A Norfolk Gallery
Faber 1948

Lewis, George
A Life of Joseph Hall DD Bishop of Exeter and Norwich
Hodder & Stoughtom 1886

Plunketts, The
Website administered by Jonathan Plunkett

Rye, Walter
A History of the Parish of Heigham
Roberts & Co. Norwich 1917

Welbank, Paul
The Parish of Heigham
Welbank Website, owned and managed by Paul Welbank

Wilson, Jim (Editor)
900 Years - Norwich Cathedral & Diocese
Jarrold 1996

Also by this author:
Berwick, David A.
Beating the Bounds in Georgian Norwich. Larks Press (2007)

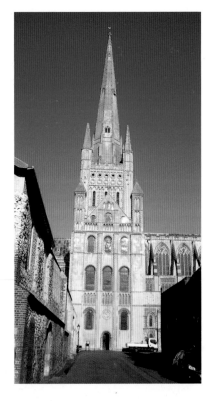

The imposing South front of Norwich Cathedral